DAIRY DEVELOPMENT IN INDIA

About the Authors

V. Venkatasubramanian, is presently working as Sr. Scientist (Agricultural Extension) and Officer-in-Charge KVK-C.T.R.I., Rajahmundry. He got his masters and doctoral degree in the field of Dairy Extension Education from National Dairy Research Institute (ICAR), Karnal and received Gold Medal for his toppership in the Master and Doctoral Programmes. Apart from his life membership in ten professional societies, he is also associated with several National and International developmental agencies as an Extension Management Specialist.

He acted as a steering committee member in the UNDP Project on Coral Reef Management and served as Editorial Board Member of the Journal of Andaman Science Association. He also served as General Secretary of the Andaman Science Association and organised national level symposiums. He has been awarded with the prestigious Young Scientists' Award for the year 1997-98 by the National Academy of Agricultural Sciences, New Delhi.

He has also received several national awards in recognition of his service. He has also invented banana fibre extraction for the benefit and farming community.

His authorship spans to more than 60 research papers, review articles and fourteen books.

A.K. Singh obtained his M.Sc. Dairying (Dairy Extension) in 1990 and Ph.D. Dairying (Dairy Extension Education) in 1995 from NDRI (ICAR).

Presently, he is working as Scientist (Ag. Extn.) in the I.A.R.I. Regional station at Indore (M.P). His work experience includes handling of Transfer of Technology projects viz. Frontline Demonstrations, Assessment and Refinement of Production Technologies, and Organization national level trainning programmes. The author has published more than 10 research papers and produced 3 Training Manuals and Extension Literature.

S.V.N. Rao is presently working as Professor and Head, Department of Veterinary and Animal Husbandry Extension at Rajiv Gandhi College of Veterinary and Animal Sciences, Pondicherry. He obtained his Master and doctoral degrees from NDRI, Karnal. During his tenure as Sr. Scientist at NDRI, he was actively involved in organising various field extension activities and teaching of post-graduate courses in extension and management. He underwent training in Extension Management and Farming Systems Research in the Netherlands and U.K. and had experience in working with Indo-Dutch Collaborative project and Indo-UK higher education link programme. Dr. Rao presented a number of papers in various national and international seminars. He has also guided M.Sc. and Ph.D. students. He has 33 research articles to his credit.

DAIRY DEVELOPMENT IN INDIA

(An Appraisal of Challenges and Achievements)

V. Venkatasubramanian
A.K. Singh
S.V.N. Rao

CONCEPT PUBLISHING COMPANY, NEW DELHI-110059

ISBN 81-8069-044-X

First Published 2003

Published and Printed by
Ashok Kumar Mittal
Concept Publishing Company
A/15-16, Commercial Block, Mohan Garden,
NEW DELHI - 110059 (India)

Phones : 25351460, 25351794
Fax : 091-11-25357103
Email : publishing@conceptpub.com

FOREWORD

The livestock economy of our country has attracted widespread attention and several organized development attempts have been made for its improvement since from the beginning of 20th century. The pace of dairy development has picked up only after 1970 with the launching of Operation Flood. If we look at the history, dairy development programmes have gone through a metamorphic change from the initial Key Village Scheme and Intensive Cattle Development Project aimed at the upgradation of local cattle to a nationwide anti-poverty programme as an instrument to social security in rural India. One cannot forget the fact that livestock sector commands greater equity at the grassroot level providing economic strength to our weaker sections. Therefore, presently dairy development component has become a part and parcel of our rural development programmes to ensure equity and food security to the weaker section through self-reliance.

The achievement made in this sector becomes insignificant if it is viewed against the present challenges faced by it. With the WTO in force, the dairy sector is open to global competition irrespective of the protective and counter vailing measures adopted by the Government. In the book the authors have summarized and discussed various challenges and opportunities in a comprehensive manner. There must be continuous flow of appropriate technologies to equip our dairy industry to face the present day challenges. The consequences of such technological introduction in the system is expected to be desirable, direct and anticipated. However, adoption of such technologies may also result in some unanticipated consequences which are indirect unexpected and undesirable to the members of the system. The cross breeding programme is no exception to this and an attempt was made to analyze both desirable and undesirable consequences experienced as a result of implementing this sensitive programme. The above analysis discussed in the book was made out of reviewing various research findings available in this direction. It is a noteworthy contribution by the authors to provide a clear-cut information about the cross breeding programme in terms of its strengths and weaknesses.

Due to the dairy co-operative movement the Indian Dairy Industry has become producer oriented and milk producers were assured of reasonable market and price. Conversion of seasonal surprises into milk powder and its recombination into liquid milk in the lean months ensured adequate returns to the farmers and an affordable consumers price. The Anand model of co-operative structure built on a vertically integrated 3-tiered structure linked the producers with urban consumers by introducing intensive milk production model, improved technology and marketing. The national policy to transfer the Anand type dairy co-operatives to other parts of India was a recognition of the importance of lessons learnt at Anand. The people involved and situations cannot be recreated as each setting is unique, but what remains is the concept of the dairy co-operatives and how it can be transplanted to other regions. The factors responsible for the success and failure of milk co-operative have been analyzed in this book by comparing the milk co-operatives of Gujarat and Haryana.

The present book has also analyzed the Strengths, Weaknesses, Opportunities and Threats of Dairy Development, which is of paramount importance. The analysis on economics of Dairy Extension and Development provides an insight about the economic viability of our projects and their possible failure due to duplications based on their initial success as pilot projects. It is indeed a pioneer effort in this direction and I congratulate the authors Dr. V. Venkatasubramanian, Dr. S.V. N. Rao and Dr. A.K. Singh for their whole hearted efforts in this task. The book is not only informative but also comprehensive in its coverage. I wish every success to the authors and the publishers for bringing out this piece of work on Dairying in the form of a book.

(B.N. Mathur)

Director, National Dairy Research Institute
(Indian Council of Agricultural Research), Karnal (Haryana)

PREFACE

India through its systematic planning in the form of various Dairy Development programmes has reached the present Milk Production level of 84 million tonnes topping the world in terms of Milk Products. The present achievement is the fruitful culmination of the sustained, systematic and intensive efforts made by the Government of India through its various cattle development programmes over the years. The Milk Production system in the rural India through the implementation of operation flood series has been further strengthened and resulted in the establishment of national milk grid. Even though, India has made remarkable strides in the arena of dairy development, the achievement is considered insignificant when it is viewed against the challenges and constraints faced by the dairy sector. The root cause of many of these constraints are too many bovines, paucity of funds, heavy pressure of human population, and to some extent the socio-economic conditions of our farmers.

The pace of dairy development has picked up only after 1970 with the launching of Operation Flood series. The Anand Model co-operatives are successful in few States and they could not prove their mettle in other States of the country especially in major milk producing States like Uttar Pradesh, Punjab and Haryana. All these aspects of our dairy development programmes needs a thorough understanding and warrants an in-depth analysis.

The strengths, weaknesses, opportunities and threats associated with the Dairy Development need to be analysed to know about the reality which helps for a better planning. Some of the dairy development programmes like crossbreeding our native cattle with exotic breeds, neglecting of buffaloes have generated lot of controversies. In this context an attempt has been made in this book to analyse various development issues related to dairy development for the benefit of dairy development professionals.

The chapters in the book are presented in two parts. Part one gives an overview of development and challenges of Indian dairying, consequences of the crossbreeding programme and SWOT analysis of dairy development. Part two comprises of three chapters dealing with management of dairy development agencies, analysis of success and failure of milk co-operatives and issues related to dairy extension and development. Relevant information on each of the above aspects of the dairying have been collected and critically viewed for creating a scientific base to carry out further research and development in the field of dairying. It gives the foresight and considerable evidence of pros and cons with respect to dairy development in the country.

This book is primarily meant for researchers, teachers, professionals involved in the dairy development work and policy makers concerned with the dairy research, development and planning.

We hope that the discussion made in the book will help the readers to understand various aspects of Indian Dairying in a most comprehensive and critical way to face the present and future challenges in the field.

We acknowledge with thanks for the sincere efforts taken by Shri Vignesh Prints, Chennai to typeset and design the manuscripts. We express our gratitude and thanks to Mr. Ashok Kumar Mittal, Concept Publishing Company for bringing out the book in the present form in the hands of the readers.

10th July, 2002

V. Venkatasubramanian
A.K. Singh
S.V.N. Rao

CONTENTS

PART - II

MANAGEMENT IN DAIRY DEVELOPMENT PROGRAMMES

LIST OF TABLES

PART I

ISSUES OF DAIRY DEVELOPMENT PROGRAMMES

1

INDIAN DAIRYING
Development and Challenges

India through its systematic planning in the form of various Dairy Development programmes has reached the present milk production level of 84 million tonnes topping the world in terms of milk production. The importance of livestock in Indian agricultural economy has been well recognised and next to land and irrigation, livestock is the single largest productive asset in rural India. The All India Debt and Investment Survey (1981) has reported that about 75 per cent of the Indian rural households were keeping the livestock and the average value of these livestock has been estimated as Rs. 2500 per livestock rearing household. On the basis of the data collected across the country it is estimated that the average value of the livestock kept by the livestock rearing family units is Rs 5,800. Uneven distribution of the livestock value across the State clearly indicated the prevalence of a wide gap between the resource rich livestock owners and the average livestock farmers. Few States like Haryana, Punjab, Gujarat, Tamil Nadu, Andhra Pradesh, Karnataka, Maharashtra, Uttar Pradesh and Maharashtra accounts for more than 70 per cent of the cattle economy in the country.

The estimated value of livestock holding of the rural population was at Rs. 168 billion during 1986 and presently it is Rs. 225 billion with an estimated contribution of 12 per cent to the country's gross domestic product (GoI, 1989 and 1990). Among the livestock, cattle and buffalo together accounted for 90 per cent of the livestock wealth in the country during 1978 (RBI, 1978) and at present it has decreased to 72 per cent. Due to the commercialised growth of poultry sector with its short term return during eighties and nineties the poultry sector has achieved a phenomenal growth rate of 70 per cent and presently occupying about 22 per cent of the country's livestock wealth.

Bullocks are the primary source of draught power in agriculture. He-buffaloes are used for draught purposes only to a limited extent and that too in certain ecological zones. Cows are numerically preponderant among milk animals, but, because of their low productivity account for only 46 per cent of the milk output. On the other hand the she-buffaloes which account for only 33 per cent of milk animals population in the country yield to 54 per cent of the total milk production. During 1985 the buffaloes contribution to total milk production was 57 per cent and with the increase in crossbreds population and intensive upgradation of the native germ-plasm the contribution of the white cattle has increased from 43 per cent to 46 per cent and if the same trend continues it may equate with the buffalo by at least 2020.

Dairy Development : An Overview

The present achievement in the India's milk production is the fruitful culmination of the sustained, systematic and intensive efforts made by the GoI through its various cattle development programmes over years. The milk production system in the rural India through the implementation of Operation Flood series has been further strengthened and resulted in the establishment of national milk grid. In the initial phase though the contribution of bovines to the national economy was significant the productivity per animal was very low in comparison to production parameters of the exotic animals. According to the estimates furnished by FAO during 1978, the World average annual milk yield per cow in milk was about 1964 kg and the estimated milk yield per cow in India during the corresponding period was 486 kg which was one of the lowest in the world. During that period, the average yield per cow for Asia as a whole was 698 kg (FAO, 1978). It has been diagnosed that inferior genetic quality and low level of feeding are the two major factors responsible for the low productivity of our stock and consequently planwise cattle development programmes have been launched. The above efforts have resulted with the present improved production level of stock with an average milk yield level of 895 kg per lactation (Venkatasubramanian and Fulzele, 1996). The present achievement is significantly low if we compare the milk animals in developed countries. Taking into the larger dimensions of our cattle holdings and the innumerable socio-cultural problems associated thereof if we estimate the average productivity of our improved stock alone leaving the indigenous unproductive animals and buffaloes our achievement over the years is plausible and the average production per improved breed of cattle comes around 1261 kg per lactation. This gives a satisfaction to the extent that if not full the achievement made hitherto is not less than remarkable. For the general information of the readers a brief account of the cattle development programmes implemented in the country over years has been discussed in this chapter.

From the beginning of this century the livestock economy of this country has attracted widespread attention and several development attempts have been made for its improvement. The British Administration has formed several committees to understand the features of livestock farming system and ways for its development. Among the various committees and their reports, the reports submitted by the Royal Commission on Agriculture (RCA) and W.A. Burns report on the Technological Possibilities of Agricultural Development in India (1944) are considered significant. However, the pre-independence attempts on livestock development were limited in scale and geographical coverage. These attempts did not have any follow-up action and lacks specificity in terms of programme planning and implementation. The above constraints in the livestock development has been done away through the introduction of planning in the post-independence period which emphasised a systematic and intensive approach.

Key Village Scheme (KVS) and Intensive Cattle Development Project (ICDP)

To start with the Key Village Scheme operation during the first three Five Year Plan periods and out of the experience learnt from KVS, the Intensive Cattle Development Project has been introduced in sixties. The KVS has initially concentrated on establishing the bull breeding farms in the major cattle tracts of the country. The initial phase of this programme was very much general in approach and no serious thought was given to improve the productivity of the stock as the bull stations established mainly constituted the local stocks than the breeds selected out for their productive traits. The other aspects of cattle development such as nutrition, fodder development, disease prevention and health care were not given any attention and as a result the KVS could not be able to achieve any breakthrough during the first phase of its inception.

On realisation of the above lacuna the KVS was transformed into an integrated and comprehensive programme with an aim and intention to improve the productivity of cattle by including the hitherto neglected aspects of cattle development such as scientific management practices, and organised marketing facilities. By the end of Second Plan 612 KVS centres were functioning in the country and an official review of the project in 1961 has been conducted and the review report severely indicated and condemned the scheme for its limited coverage (10 per cent of total stock) and insignificant contribution (GoI, Ministry of Agriculture, 1962).

Since the KVS could not be able to produce the expected and desirable change in the cattle development, the GoI has come out with a more comprehensive and intensive development alternative to KVS by implementing the Intensive Cattle Development Project (ICDP). The ICDP has been given a serious thrust to meet the growing urban demand of milk and to feed the public sector dairy plants through increasing the milk production of our cattle. It is at this juncture the low level milk producing capacity of our indigenous milk breeds and their crosses to meet the growing demand has been felt seriously and consequently great emphasis has been placed on cross-breeding of our native cows with exotic dairy breeds like Holstein-Freision, Jersey and Brown Swiss as per their agroclimatic suitabilities. In addition, the disease prevention, health care and nutritional management aspects have been given a renewed importance than the KVS. Therefore, the launch of ICDP is thus distinguished the KVS by inclusion of cross-breeding component, integrated livestock management and linking up with rural dairying with the urban milk supply. Each ICDP area or Block has been entrusted with a target population of one lakh cow and she-buffalo population. The scheme also provided with all necessary inputs and services simultaneously required to milk producers. At the end of 1960, a total of 62 ICDP centres were in operation throughout the country and in those ICDP areas where the KVS were functioning, it has been merged with the ICDP.

Operation Flood

The pace of dairy development in India has picked up only after 1970 with the launching of Operation Flood. This period has also seen the emergence of dairy co-operatives as the dominant force. The milk producers have been assured with reasonable markets and dairy industry has become producer oriented. Presently, India has emerged as the world's largest producer of milk and become a model for other countries with respect to its Anand model milk cooperative system. The first phase of the Operation Flood Programme (OF-I) was operated between 1970 and 1981. It envisaged a concentrated effort to increase the milk output in 27 milk sheds located in the hinterlands of the four metropolitan cities, viz. New Delhi, Mumbai, Kolkata and Chennai. The funds needed for its implementation were generated by the sale of donated stock of butter oil and skimmed milk powder after recombination into milk for the benefit of Indian urban population. These aid commodities were freely given by European Economic Communities (EEC) from its surplus stocks as an aid through World Food Programme (WFP) of the United Nations.

Initially, the Operation Flood-I has covered eight rural districts and later on extended to 27 districts with a participation of 1.4 million rural families. The second phase of the Operation Flood was launched in 1982 and was scheduled to be completed by 1985. The Operation Flood-II was to link 147 major towns, 160 districts with a financial outlay of Rs. 4800 million, it is one of the biggest dairy development projects ever undertaken in India (National Dairy Development Board, 1979). The main objectives of the project are:

(a) To build up the infrastructure for the development of a growing and self-reliant dairy industry consisting of 10 million rural families of milk producers and a national milk herd of about 14 million crossbred cows and she-buffaloes by 1980s;
(b) To link up the rural supply sources and urban demand centres (with a population of 150 million) through establishment of appropriate marketing arrangements; and
(c) To increase the per capita consumption of milk in the national diet.

The Operation Flood-II was financially supported by both the EEC (dairy commodities aid) and the World Bank (financial aid). In 1986, the Operation Flood-III was proposed by the Government of India to the EEC and World Bank to further extend and consolidate the dairy development in the country by strengthening the grassroot level infrastructure facilities for milk procurement, milk processing and marketing networks established under Operation Flood-I and II. The Operation Flood-III was proposed up to 1994 which is mainly intended to cover the imbalances remaining after Operation Flood-I and II with a coverage to additional 15,000 villages and 200 medium size urban centres. The Operation Flood Programmes thus have been implemented with the aids and grants received from World Food Programme (WFP) of the United Nations Food and Agricultural Organisation (FAO), the European Economic Community (EEC) and the World Bank. The WFP has supported the Operation Flood (1970-81) with its dairy commodity aid and financial grant involving a total outlay of nearly Rs. 1,200 million and Operation Flood-II and III have involved an outlay of Rs. 4855 million and Rs. 6,806 million respectively. Out of the total funds received about one-third of the total cost of these projects have been funded by World Bank and rest (about 50 per cent) originated in the form of dairy commodity aid from European Economic Community.

The Operation Flood Programmes by and large differed from the ICDP that they laid emphasis on milk supply and marketing schemes and viewed dairy development as an instrument for rural development and social change. This is because of the realisation of the fact that the growth of dairying requires apart from the increase in milk production, the milk production centres need to be linked with marketing centres to ensure the farmers and customers their fair deal and to create a sustainable strong base for the dairy development in the country. The Operation Flood part of the dairy development has clearly emphasised the social aspects of developing through the importance given for the establishment and growth of Village Milk Producers Cooperative Societies (VMPCSs) throughout the country followed by the initial success of Anand Milk Producers Union in uplifting the farmers. The details of the growth of Anand Pattern Village Milk Producers Co-operative Societies during the Operation Flood Programmes is given hereunder.

Growth of Village Milk Producers' Co-operative and Procurement under Operation Flood (1970 to 1990)

Year	Member VMPCS	Annual Milk Producers ('000)	Procurement (million tonnes)
OF-I			
1970-71	1588	278	0.1898
1971-72	1811	327	0.2372
1972-73	2200	361	0.2774
1973-74	2598	394	0.2226
1974-75	2966	445	0.3175
1975-76	4533	562	0.4197
1976-77	7681	723	0.5657
1977-78	9306	943	0.6205
1978-79	10099	1213	0.7336
1979-80	11436	1475	0.8614
1980-81	13270	1747	0.9844
OF-II			
1981-82	18422	2124	1.0147
1982-83	23496	2620	1.6133
1983-84	28614	3116	1.9016
1984-85	34523	3632	2.1097
OF-III			
1985-86	42692	4484	2.8762
1986-87	49077	5097	2.8652
1987-88	54525	5666	2.8105
1988-89	58883	6250	2.9090
1989-90	60825	7003	3.5821

Thus, it is clearly evident that the dairy development programme in the country has gone through a metamorphic change from the initial Key Village Scheme and Intensive Cattle Development Project aimed at the upgradation of local cattle in selected tracts to a nationwide anti-poverty programme as an instrument to social security in the rural India.

In the meantime, in 1989 Technology Mission on Dairy Development was launched to augment the rural income through the application of modern technologies in dairying. It also emphasised the optimisation of resource use for cattle improvement in terms of breeding farms, bull mother farms, semen freezing and artificial insemination facilities, veterinary health care facilities etc. available with the State animal husbandry departments and under Operation Flood. In addition, the research establishments under the Indian Council of Agriculture Research (ICAR) and State Agricultural Universities (SAUs) have also been linked up in the process to provide the research/technological support. Presently, the dairy development component has become a part of the countries rural development programmes with its extension to schemes like Training of Rural Youth to Self Employment (TRYSEM), Integrated Rural Development Programme (IRDP), Small Farmer Development Agency (SFDA), Tribal Welfare Programmes etc. to ensure food security to the weaker sections through self-reliance.

THE CHALLENGES

Even though, India has made remarkable strides in the arena of dairy development, the achievement is considered insignificant when it is viewed against the challenges faced by the dairy sector. Huge cattle and buffalo population in the country, very low per capita availability of milk, very low productivity of milch animals, huge expenditure involved in planning and implementing various dairy development projects, tremendous increase in foodgrain and oilseed production, under utilization of the large installed capacities of dairy plants and the fact that a large number of population cannot be offered to consume milk are some of the challenges faced by the country in terms of its dairy development. The researchers have identified a number of challenges which were summarised and discussed in this part under the following sub-heads for the purpose of brevity and clarity.

(1) Socio-economic challenges,
(2) Research and Extension,
(3) Milk Procurement and Processing, and
(4) Organisational Challenges.

Socio-Economic Challenges

The dairy development in the country is hamstrung by its characteristic socio-economic situations. In addition to the ever increasing human and animal population, a number of other factors are decelerating the pace of dairy development in the country. They are:

(i) Small and Scattered Herds

Out of about 98 million farm holdings in the country over 75 million are owning land below 2 ha. This is in addition to about 30 per cent of the rural families who are landless (Patel, 1993). Dairy production is largely taken up as a subsidiary occupation to crop production in rural areas.

(ii) Investment in Dairying

The investment in dairying has decreased from 0.82 per cent of the total Plan expenditure in First Plan to 0.58 per cent in the Seventh Plan, whereas the value of output from the dairying increased from Rs. 6500 million in 1951 to Rs. 2,60,000 millicn in 1990 (Economic Survey, 1990-91, National Accounts Statistics, 1991, Planning Commission, Ministry of Agricultural Annual Reports, *Dairy India*, 1992). It is clear from these figures that the expenditure on AH and Dairying is very much out of proportion to their importance in the economy of the country.

The paucity of funds is a serious constraint which impedes investment in manpower development, creation of proper communication, infrastructure, establishing reliable data base and strengthening the extension network in the villages.

Research and Extension

Research and extension provide support to agricultural development. Investment in agricultural research in the country have increased steadily over the years. There must be a continuous flow of technologies to suit the requirements of the changing situations in the dairy farming. It is one of the requirements for agricultural development. However, it is not always possible for the researchers to offer solutions to each and every problem. At any point of time the research:

- Has offered solutions to problems which may or may not be adopted by the farmers.
- Is trying to modify or refine the solutions to suit the requirements of the farmers.
- Is concentrating its efforts on future problems.

Though applied research is trying to find solutions for field problems, one has to realise that certain things are unsurmountable for research. For Instance,

- To produce humped animals through cross-breeding.
- Enriching or treating straws to get feeds equivalent to the quality of berseem.
- Maintaining heterogenity at higher levels of exotic inheritance.
- Obtaining only female crossbred calves through Artificial Insemination (A.I.).
- Instrument to predict or detect heat in animals.
- Evolving cows which can produce milk continuously.
- Developing economical milk chilling unit for rural areas.
- Developing a method for SNF testing in milk at field level.

Conflicting Goals for the Policy Makers, Researchers, Extension Personnel and Farmers

Though all these groups of people directly or indirectly work for increasing agricultural production in the country, quite often the means to achieve this goal vary and create confusion. Policy makers are usually interested in populist measures which may or may not contribute to agricultural production. For Instance, the Integrated Rural Development Programme initiated by the Government of India, was found to be a drain on economy.

Extension workers concentrate on large farmers to achieve the targets (number of cows inseminated rather than number of beneficiaries) in short duration by expending less energy. Input suppliers aim at profit by supplying inputs to few bulk consumers rather than spending time and other resources in covering more number of small farmers.

The researchers are basically interested in developing the technologies for satisfying the need for publications which are usually linked to their career advancement. These technologies were developed mainly because the researchers, extension workers and farmers operate in isolation and as such the researchers may not be aware of the needs as perceived by the farmers. Many a time the research is being conducted on research stations for the interest of large farmers. Hence, many of the technologies developed are more applicable to the resource rich farmers rather than to a large number of small and marginal farmers who need the research support more.

In addition, doubts are also expressed about the adequacy of the present system of extension, ability of the extension workers in absorbing and communicating the modern technologies to the farmers in an understandable form and the capability of the research system to communicate the multi-crop, multi-animal, multi-disciplinary knowledge down the lane.

Constraints related to Breeding

Systematic introduction of exotic inheritance into local stock has proved to be a better alternative to increasing milk production in the country. Most of the States have implemented cross breeding programme with Jersey, Holstein-Friesian, Red Dane and Brown Swiss breeds. The performance of the crossbreds maintained under the village conditions was not quite encouraging compared to those under organised farms.

The major constriants observed in cross-breeding were low reproductive performance through artificial insemination, high incidence of repeat breeding in crossbreds, indiscriminate breeding and slaughtering of high yielding animals, ill equipped A.I. Centres and inadequate expert services.

Prejudice against crossbred males as draught animals and the differences in the performance of the crossbred and indigenous males forced the farmers to have a negative attitude towards the crossbred males. In addition, the value of a crossbred bullock compared to indigenous bullock is very low and the farmer requires more feed than the latter.

Ill-defined and less detailed breeding policy with respect to different regions in the country, socio-economic factors of the farmers and non-availability of the recorded population of pedigreed females were some of the factors which constrains the cross-breeding programme. Though a number of negative consequences were associated with the cross-breeding technology, higher demands for animal products probably justify its implementation.

Upgrading of buffaloes with Murrah, Mehsana and other good' breeds is accepted as a policy to improve their productivity. However, the low conception rate in buffaloes through A.I. is posing lot of problems in implementing this policy. In addition, the problem of identifying buffaloes in heat by the farmers is also a serious hindcrance to the Artificial Insemination (A.I.) Programme in buffaloes.

Constraints in Feeding of Livestock

Balanced feeding of dairy animals is the basis for successful dairy farming. A profitable dairy must have animals with a high genetic potential for milk production, which are fed on least cost balanced ration to achieve the most economical milk output. Imbalance or shortage in the supply of essential nutrients, energy and protein results in poor performance on growth, reproduction and milk production. Constraints related to feeding revolve around the price and availability of feeds and fodders. Poor availability and lack of quality feeds often resulted in the increase in feed cost and reduction in quantity fed to the animals. High cost of the concentrate feeds and irregular supply by the dairy cooperatives and other agencies often makes the farmers to prefer the locally available feeds which are inferior in quality. This was mainly due to the inadequate knowledge of the farmers about balanced feed and feeding practices.

In view of the scarcity of quality green fodder and concentrates majority of the animals are being fed on poor quality roughages which in turn reflect upon their poor health and low milk production. Efforts to improve the quality of low grade roughages through chemical and biological treatments did not yield a satisfactory technology which finds favour with the farmers.

Constraints in Disease Prevention and Control

The Government of India is implementing a number of programmes to increase the productivity per livestock unit. The animal must be in good health to produce or to work upto its full capacity. In this context disease prevention and its control assumes significance in dairy development.

Facilities for prevention as well as treatment of animal diseases must be accessible to the farmers to reduce the mortality and morbidity of our livestock. Though, a number of veterinary institutions are established to cater to the needs of the dairy farmers, it was reported by NCA way back in 1976 that most of the institutions are starved of proper equipments and medicines. Lack of these inputs naturally are a hinderance to the effective functioning of veterinarians.

At times the non-cooperation of villagers which might be because of taboos and superstitious beliefs itself is a serious constraint to the field staff in implementing the disease control programmes.

An efficient disease reporting system and follow-up

action is necessary for the effective prevention and control of animal diseases. Lack of proper reporting and surveillance is a serious constraint experienced by the veterinary professionals which led to the trial and error *modus operandi* in treatment of animals. Inadequate vaccine supply and the difficulty in restricting the animal movement were also reported as serious constraints experienced by the field staff of Dairy Cooperative Federation.

For an effective and efficient disease control system apart from the inbuilt disease reporting system, regular supply of the vaccines, medicines and restriction of animal movements during the disease outbreaks are more important.

Milk Procurement and Processing

At present milk is being processed in the dairies under government, private and co-operative sectors. It is stated that not more than 20 per cent of the milk is being handled by this organised sector. The private dairies are mostly involved in the manufacture of milk products with little or no attention to the supply of fluid milk to the consumers. Wherever the private dairies are existing the government and co-operative dairies are facing stiff competition in milk procurement as well as sale of products such as ghee and skimmed milk powder. Incidentally, many of these private dairies are located in the north-western part of the country. With the delicensing policy of the government many more dairies are entering into the fray in private sector. These private dairies are concentrating on collecting buffalo milk which is required for manufacturing products. Very little attention is being paid to increase milk production, produce clean milk or procure hygienic milk. As a result, many dairies are incurring losses due to spoilages.

The absence of regular and remunerative market for milk and milk products is a major constraints encountered by the farmers. Lack of or inadequate credit facilities to the farmers for dairy purpose and exploitation by the middlemen hampers the farmer from deriving maximum profit from dairying.

Similarly, there are no organized markets for fodders and animals in the country.

Organisational Challenges

At present the dairy development activities are being carried out by national level organizations such as NDDB, ICAR and its institutes, and State level organizations like milk federations, animal husbandry departments and non-government organizations. The success of these organizations in achieving their objectives depends upon the availability of funds, morale and capabilities of their employees and policies of the organization.

It is not out of place to mention here that there is nothing like dairy extension personnel solely responsible for the education of dairy farmers. Dairy extension activity is always treated as secondary to many other activities such as milk procurement in case of milk union employees and treatment and insemination of animals by Animal Husbandry personnel. The net result is that majority of the farmers are not aware of the concepts of dairy farming and also of the facilities available to them by various organizations.

Some of the significant organizational and administrative constraints reported by the research workers were inadequate staff, lack of facilities and opportunities for training of the personnel and lack of incentives for good work. Lack of technical manpower to manage various levels of dairy development activities was reported as a serious constraint that impedes dairy development.

The other constraints experienced by veterinarians and the farmers were improper location of the veterinary dispensaries, inadequate communication and transportation facilities. The distant location of dairy development units is a disincentive for the farmers to avail the facilities such as A.I. (Artificial Insemination), Veterinary aid etc. This is especially true with landless and other resource poor farmers who cannot afford to lose wages for half a day, the time required to take their sick animals to distantly located veterinary institutions for treatment. As a sequel these farmers prefer natural service over A.I. and treatment by quack rather than veterinarian because of their easy accessibility even at odd hours.

Less promotional opportunities, poor pay scales, lack of career advancement and special allowances for working in odd hours, absence of incentives and awards for good work were some of the serious constraints experienced by the field workers. More emphasis on submission of reports and record maintenance force the field staff to devote more time for paper work at the cost of other important activities.

The country cannot afford to give technical inputs and services free of cost to the farmers. It is high time that the farmers must share the expenditure involved on inputs and services. The developmental organizations must aim at providing quality inputs and services by charging the farmers. It has the following advantages:

— The demand for quality inputs and services will increase.
— There will be proper utilization of the inputs and the services.
— It provides for proper maintenance of records and accountability of the staff.
— The farmers start realising the value of the technology.

Though, NCA (1976) has recommended to charge the farmers for A.I. in areas where it is more popular, it is still being offered free of cost or at a nominal price in many parts of the country. Therefore, the practice of providing free services to the farmers need to be reviewed for a policy change.

Summary

It can be concluded that low milk production in the country is constrained because of various factors. These constriants influence the milk production of animals either singly or in combination, depending upon the farming system location. Some constraints such as disposal of male crossbred animals, milk prices etc. require policy interventions whereas some other constraints like low conception rate, improving the quality of feeds need research and extension interventions. Education of farmers on various aspects of dairy farming coupled with creation of proper infrastructure facilities help in increasing the adoption of technologies. However, care need to be taken in identification of suitable farming system locations while introducing the technologies.

The root causes of many of these constraints are too many bovines, paucity of funds, illiteracy of farmers and pressure of human population. It calls for a thorough discussion on the part of the policy makers, scientists, extension personnel, and input suppliers of various organizations including non-government organizations and farmers to address these constraints which may vary from place to place in their intensity. Use of Participatory Rural Appraisal may help not only in the identification of problems but also in finding suitable solutions. A well co-ordinated effort on the part of the concerned organizations associated with the dairy development programmes either directly or indirectly go a long way at least in mitigating these constraints if not eliminating them *in toto*.

References

Acharya, R.M. (1984). Constraints in Milk Production Enhancement in India, *Diamond Jubilee Souvenir* (1983-84), NDRI, Karnal.

Acharya, R.M. (1989). Cross Breeding Cattle as an Instrument to Increase Milk Production in Rural Areas, *Indian J. Anim. Sci.*, 59 (2) : 264.

Acharya, R.M. (1990). Promise of White Revolution, Key Note Address Delivered at 15th Dairy Husbandry Officers Workshop, NDRI, Karnal.

Chambers, R. and Jiggins, J. (1986). *Agricultural Research for Resource Poor Farmers : A Parsimonious Paradigm*, IDS, Sussex, England.

Chander, S. (1970). A Study of Socio-economical Factors Affecting the Adoption of Artificial Iinsemination and Attitude of Farmers Towards the Same, M.Sc. thesis, Panjab University, Chandigarh.

George, P.S. and Nair, K.N. (1990). *Livestock Economy of Kerala*, Centre for Development Studies, Trivandrum.

Ghosh, D.K. (1991). Making IRDP Investment Efficient, *Kurukshetra*, Dec., 19-23.

Ghosh, D.K. (1993). TRYSEM and Voluntary Action, *Kurukshetra*, Sep., 29.

Gill, C.S. (1979). Retrospects and Prospects of Cross Breeding for Dairy Cattle Improvement in India, *Indian Dairyman*, 31(2):83.

Giridhar, P.N. (1967). *A Study of Factors Resorting the Progress of Artificial Insemination in Haryana*, M.Sc. thesis, Panjab Agricultural University, Hissar.

Gupta, K.K. and De, Dipak (1989). A Comparative Study on Constraints Perceived by Adopters and Non-adopters in Rearing Crossbred Cows in Jaipur District, Rajasthan, *Indian J. Dairy Sci.*, 42(3):456.

Jose, T.K. (1988). Dairying in Kerala, 22nd Dairy Industry Conference, Trivandrum, 29.

Mosher, A.T. (1966). Conditions to be Met to Accelerate Agricultural Development, Agricultural Development Council, New York.

Nataraju, M.S. and Channegowda, M.S. (1986). Some Aspects about Adopters of Dairy Innovations, *Dairy Guide*, 8(2) : 47.

Nayak, H.S.; Bajaj, S.S. and Raut, D.R. (1986). Problems of Dairy Farmers in Ahmednagar District of Maharashtra, *Maha. J. Extn. Edu.*, 5 : 107.

National Commission on Agriculture 1976. *Animal Husbandry,* Part VII, Ministry of Food and Agriculture, Government of India, New Delhi.

Patel, R.K. (1993). Present Status and Promise of Dairying in India, *Indian Dairyman*, 45 (7) : 276.

Patel, R.K.; Singh, C.B.; Sharma, P.A. and Mahipal (1978). Constraints in Transfer and Adoption of New Technologies, Operational Research Project Report, NDRI, Karnal, 117.

Patel, S.M.; Thakur, D.S. and Pandey, M.K. (1979). *Impact of Milk Cooperatives in Gujarat*, United Publishers, Allahabad.

Rao, M.R. and Sastri, P.M. (1984). Prospects and Constraints in Milk Production Programmes through the Weaker Sections of the Rural Society, *Indian Dairyman*, 36(9) : 481.

Rao, M.V. (1993). Issue Paper on National Agricultural Technology Project, Andhra Pradesh Agricultural University, Hyderabad.

Rao, B.S. (1987). *A Study of Transfer of Dairy Production Technologies in Chittoor District of Andhra Pradesh*, Ph.D. thesis, Kurukshetra University, Kurukshetra.

Rao, S.V.N.; Venkatasubramanian, V. and Rao, B.S (1995). Constraints of Dairy Development in India. *Indian Journal of Animal Production and Management*, 11(4) : 177-185.

Rao, S.V.N; Venkatasubramanian, V. and Jandevit (1995). Consequences of Cross-breeding Programme in India, *Economic and Political Weekly* 30(39) : 112-116.

Rath, B.B. (1977). *A Critical Analysis of Intensive Cattle Development Project: Progress, Problems and Prospects*, Ph.D. thesis, Haryana Agricultural University, Hissar.

Saini, S.P.S. (1975). *A Study of Factors Affecting Adoption of Selected Recommended Practices*, M.Sc. thesis, Punjab Agricultural University, Ludhiana.

Sharma, R.K. (1967). *A Study into the Impediments in Contagious Bovine Diseases and Control Work in Hissar District*, M.Sc. thesis, Haryana Agricultural University, Hissar.

Sharma, R.K. (1977). Problems and Prospects of Livestock Development, *Haryana Review*, 11(7) : 10.

Sharma, R.K. (1980). *A Study of Socio-Psychological and Infrastructural Constraints in the Efficient Execution of ICDP*, Ph.D. thesis, Kurukshetra University, Kurukshetra.

Sharma, R.K. (1985). Intensive Cattle Development Project: A Constraint Prone and Inadequate Services Support Programme, *J. Extn. Systems*, 1:75.

Sharma, R.K. and Makhija, V.K. (1991). Constraints Encountered by Field Veterinarians in Implementing the Programmes of ICDP, *Indian J. Dairy Sci.*, 49(7).

Singhal, S.P. (1979). Artificial Insemination under Field Condition: Problems and Solutions, *Livestock Adviser*, 4(2).

Singh, D. (1978). Problems of Transfer of Technology, in Transfer of Technology Systems and Constraints, U.P. Society of Extension Education and Rural Development, Institute of Agricultural Sciences, Kanpur.

Singh, S.; Raut, K.C. and Jain, J.P. (1986). Performance of Cross-bred Cows *vis-a-vis* Non-descripts in a Hilly Area of Himachal Pradesh, *Indian J. Anim. Sci.*, 56 (5) : 542.

Singh, V. (1984). *Impact of Mini Dairy Scheme in District Karnal* (Haryana), M.Sc. thesis, Kurukshetra University, Kurukshetra.

Sohal, T.S. and Rao, S.V.N. (1986). Mechanism of Accelerating Transfer of Dairy Farming Technology, *Dairy Guide*, 8 (9) : 17.

Staempfli, H.; Valiathan Unnikrishan, V.S. and Kuepfer, K. (1984). Fertility of Cattle Kept Under Village Conditions in Kerala, *Indian Dairyman*, 36:69.

Tomar, N.S. (1979). Problems and Prospects of Artificial Inseminations under Field Conditions, presented at 7th North-West Dairy Husbandry Officers' Workshop held at NDRI, Karnal.

Vaidyanathan, A. (1989). *Research on the Livestock Economy : An Overview in Livestock Economy of India*, Indian Society of Agricultural Economics, Oxford and IBH Publishing Co., New Delhi.

Venkatasubramanian, V. and Ramachand (1990). Infrastructural and Recognition Constraints by Field Veterinarians of Tamil Nadu, *Cherion*, 19(4) : 177.

Venkatasubramanian, V. and Ramachand (1991). Constraints : Dairy Development in India, *Milcow*, 13(3) : 3.

Venkatasubramanian, V. and Ramachand (1993). Socio-Psychological Constraints perceived by Field Veterinarians of Tamil Nadu, *Indian Veterinary Journal*, 70 (5) : 472.

2

CONSEQUENCES OF CROSS-BREEDING PROGRAMME IN INDIA

Introduction

Cross-breeding with exotic dairy cattle has been extensively adopted since 1963. This chapter reviews the cross-breeding programmes and analyses its desirable and undesirable consequences. Consequences are the changes that occur to an individual or to a social system as a result of the adoption or rejection of an innovation/technology. The technologies are often introduced into the system with the expectation that the consequences will be desirable, direct and anticipated. However, adoption of such technologies may result in some unanticipated consequences which can be indirect and undesirable for the members of the system (Rogers, 1983). Cross-breeding technology is no exception to this. In this chapter, an attempt is made to analyse both desirable as well as undesirable consequences as a result of the implementation of cross-breeding programme in India.

Cross-breeding with exotic dairy breeds in cattle was introduced in the country to increase milk production through rapid improvement in the germ-plasm of our native breeds. Though, introduced in India in the beginning of this century it was implemented on a large scale with the introduction of Intensive Cattle Development Project (ICDP) in 1963 as a part of Special Development Programme in Third Five-Year Plan period.

Currently cross-breeding is being implemented through

a number of Artificial Insemination (AI) centres under the State animal husbandry departments, milk federations, voluntary organisations and organised dairy farms and universities. It was reported that every year about 12.75 million inseminations with exotic bull semen were being done by all the AI centres in the country. All these efforts led to the production of about 8.8 million cross-bred cattle and the contribution of these animals to the milk pool was not as significant as it was expected (Nair, 1989). However, Dhas (1991) reported that the preparation of cross-bred cows as the milch animal herd is one of the factors which played a dominant role in rapid increase in the milk production of Kerala.

The information of cross-bred cattle population was made available for the first time through quinquennial livestock census conducted in 1982. The census figures (Table 2.1) indicated that cross-bred population constituted about 4.6 per cent of the total cattle population in the country. Two States, Uttar Pradesh and Kerala accounted for about 50 per cent of the country's total cross-bred population. It is fascinating to observe that a large number of indigenous cattle were replaced by cross-breds in Kerala up to the tune of 46 per cent which was further increased to 56 per cent by 1990.

Cross-Breeding Policies

Cross-breeding programme has generated a lot of controversy since its inception. The literature is full of arguments in favour and against the implementation of this sensitive programme in India. It used to be at the cross roads on a number of occasions whenever the programme was slated for discussion. For almost a century, our planners tried to find answers for the following two questions: (i) Whether cross-breeding is to be implemented on a mass scale and if so in which regions? (ii) What type of B taurus breed is to be used and what should be the most optimum level of exotic inheritance?

The Royal Commission of Agriculture (RCA) appointed

Table 2.1. Percentage of Cross-breds to Total Cattle

State	Cross-breds	Indigenous	Total	(Per cent) Cross-breds
AP	173	13047	13220	1.31
Assam	145	660.5	67.50	2.15
Bihar	151	16062	1621.3	0.93
Gujarat	53	6941	6994	0.76
Haryana	266	2076	2342	11.36
HP	124	2050	2174	5.70
J and K	163	2162	232.5	7.01
Karnataka	538	10762	11300	4.76
Kerala	145.3	1644	3097	46.92
MP	66	270.51	27117	0.24
Maharashtra	492	15670	16162	3.04
Manipur	62	685	747	8.30
Meghalaya	18	532	550	3.27
Nagaland	31	120	151	20.53
Orissa	227	12703	12930	1.76
Punjab	NA	NA	NA	NA
Rajasthan	39	13466	1350.5	0.29
Sikkim	33	140	173	19.08
Tamil Nadu	885	9480	1036.5	8.54
Tripura	36	6.44	680	5.29
Uttar Pradesh	3252	22900	261.52	12.43
West Bengal	554	15103	15657	3.54
Union territories				
A and N Islands	2	34	36	5.56
Arunachal Pradesh	0	168	168	0.00
Chandigarh	2	4	6	33.33
D and N Haveli	1	44	45	2.22
Delhi	4	48	52	7.69
Goa, Daman and Diu	3	129	132	2.27
Lakshadweep	1	2	3	33.33
Mizoram	3	46	49	6.12
Pondicherry	25	68	93	26.88
Total	**8802**	**180386**	**189188**	**4.65**

by the then Government of India in 1926 recommended that the State departments not to take up experiments on cross-breeding and confine themselves to the improvement of milking qualities of indigenous breeds like Sahiwal, Sindhi or selected strains of breeds like Haryana. The animal husbandry wing of the board of agriculture and animal husbandry in India (1940 and 1941), though feeling the urgent need to increase milk production, did not recommend cross-breeding with European breeds. The Indian Council of Agricultural Research (ICAR) based on the recommendations of Gosevasangh in 1949 recommended to develop large non-descript population into dual purpose animals combining draft and milk qualities in an optimum manner. Though the cross-breeding of Indian cattle was introduced as early as 1875, it has attracted the attention of our policy-makers and planners in the year 1961 only.

Large scale cross-breeding was opposed by various experts in the past (Oliver, 1938; Peparall, 1947). Later in 1953, Zal R. Kothavalla in the 10th meeting of animal husbandry wing recommended cross-breeding not as a policy for universal adoption; but as a policy to be adopted in areas where the improvement of indigenous cattle through grading was not possible and in areas where there was great scope for augmenting the milk output.

In 1961 the Committee set up by the Central Council of Gosamvardhana recommended that cross-breeding of cattle to be taken up intensively using two or more exotic breeds in three selected areas one each in plateau, plains and hills. Similarly, Intensive Cattle Development Projects (ICDPs) were started in 1964 as a part of the special development programmes in later half of the Third Five Year Plan. Cross-breeding of bovines through AI technique by introducing exotic breeds like Jersey, Holstein-Friesian, Brown Swiss etc. to augment the milk production and to improve the breeding efficiency of bovine was given the prime importance under ICDP.

After thoroughly reviewing the cattle breeding policy the scientific panel on animal husbandry in 1965 recommended that bulk of the exotic inheritance should be obtained through Jersey and cross-breeding with Brown-Swiss and Holstein-Freisian should be tried on a limited scale. Similar recommendations were made by the National Commission on Agriculture (NCA) in 1976. Experimentation on cross-breeding of different indigenous breeds with different exotic breeds in different parts of the country was initiated to develop a cross-bred cow to suit to our requirements. As a result a number of crossbreds were evolved with different levels of exotic inheritance including triple crosses. But the systematic efforts in a few places led to the development of new breeds such as Jersind (Allahabad Agricultural Institute), Karan Swiss, Karan Fries (National Dairy Research Institute, Karnal) and Sunandini (Kerala). Despite all these efforts and loss of valuable time, it is a pity that most of the States have no well defined breeding policy even now, regarding areas where cross-breeding is to be taken up, exotic breed to be used and optimum level of exotic inheritance (Acharya, 1989 and Rao *et al.,* 1995).

Consequences

With a view to develop a clear cut breeding policy, a number of studies were conducted to compare the performance of different crossbreds with varying levels of exotic inheritance and indigenous breeds of cattle on the basis of data obtained from organised herds maintained in different agro-climatic zones.

After a thorough review on cattle and buffalo breeding, Bhattacharya (1984) concluded that cross-bred cows are more suited for high milk production than buffaloes and the former not only produce more milk than the indigenous cattle breeds and buffaloes, but are more efficient in converting feed into milk, and thus have lower cost of milk production per litre. Similarly, Acharya (1989) and Rao *et al.* (1995) on the basis of the performance data available on cross-breds in different regions remarked that cross-breeding in cattle resulted in increased milk production and helped to a great extent in rural development.

A number of studies were conducted in the past to analyse and compare different crosses with different indigenous breeds of cattle on various parameters. Most of these studies were based on the data obtained from the organised herds. A detailed review on dairy cattle cross-breeding in the tropics is available in Cunningham and Syrstad (1987) and Venkatasubramanian and Fulzele (1996). However, there are a few studies aimed at comparing the performance of cross-breds with non-descript cattle under field conditions and this chapter limits its discussion only to these studies. In addition it does not appreciate the differences within the cross-breds as well as within the indigenous cattle. Similarly, the differences between HF cross and Sahiwal cows are smaller compared to indigenous cows but it was attempted to compare cross-breds and indigenous cows to facilitate presentation.

The data reported by various workers on comparative performance of cross-breds and indigenous cattle was compiled and presented in Table 2.2(a), (b) and (c). A glance at this table revealed that cross-breds came into first heat at an early age which ranged from 25 to 33 months compared to 38 to 41 months in indigenous cattle. Pandey and Mishra (1985) observed that about 80 per cent of the cross-breds came into first heat between two to three years as against only 50 per cent in indigenous heifers.

The conception rate through AI in cross-breds was higher than in the indigenous cattle as reported by Katpatal (1977) and Staempfli *et al.* (1984). The literature convincingly indicated that the age at first calving of cross-bred heifers under field conditions was around one year less than their indigenous counterparts (Pandey and Mishra, 1985; Singh *et al.*, 1986a and Staempfli *et al.*, 1984).

The average dry period in indigenous cows was more than six months whereas it was less than four and a half months in cross-breds (Patel *et al.*, 1980 and Vanduc and Taneja, 1984). With reference to the average calving interval substantial difference between cross-breds and indigenous cows could not be observed though the former had lesser calving intervals. All these parameters discussed above lend credence to the fact that cross-breds are superior milk producers than

Table 2.2(a) (b) (c) : Comparison of Cross-breds and Indigenous Cows on Production Parameters

Age at First heat Months		Conception Rate through AI per cent		Average Age at First Calving (Months)	
X-Bred	Indigenous	X-Bred	Indigenous	X-Bred	Indigenous
25	38	51	29 h	36.0	46.0 k
31	38	37	34 k	48.0	60.0 c
				47.7	64.0 i
				41.0	51.5 a
				27.0	36.7 l
				33.2	51.3 d

Average Dry Period (Months)		Average Calving Interval (Months)		Average Lactation Length (Months)	
X-Bred	Indigenous	X-Bred	Indigenous	X-Bred	Indigenous
2.8	6.6 e	15.2	16.7 l	12.4	10.1 e
3.8	6.5 l	8.0	18.5 k	11.0	8.6 l
				15.1	12.8 i
2.8	5.0 i	17.7	19.9 i	11.1	10.0 h
2.2	4.9 h	18.4	19.2 a	10.2	7.8 j
5.2	6.6 g	14.3	15.0 b	10.1	10.0 g
4.4	8.1 d	12.4	12.7 j	11.3	9.0 d
		15.3	16.6 g		
		15.7	17.1 d		

Average Lactation Yield (Kg)		Cost of Milk Production (Rs./Kg)		Net Income/Day (Rs.)	
X-Bred	Indigenous	X-Bred	Indigenous	X-Bred	Indigenous
2931	1134 e	1.40	2.31 j	8.31	2.76 i
1330	4.57 i	1.17	1.76 g		
2440	1830 h	2.41	3.16 h		
1964-2521	949 l				
3846	1582 j				
1558	567 g				

(a) Jose (1988), (b) Katpatal (1977), (c) Pandey and Mishra (1985), (d) Patel *et al.* (1976), (e) Patel *et al.* (1980), (f) Prasad *et al.* (1991), (g) Rao (1981), (h) Sahon and Gill (1990), (i) Singh *et al.* (1986), (j) Singh and Singh (1991), (k) Staempfli *et al.* (1984), (l) Vandec and Taneja (1984).

indigenous cows. The average figures on lactation length as reported by Patel *et al.* (1980), Vanduc and Taneja (1984) and Singh *et al.* (1986a) showed that cross-breds were at least two months more in milk than indigenous cow. The difference in the average lactation yields of cross-breds and indigenous cows was quite substantial revealing thereby that cross-breds were high milk yielders compared to indigenous cows. Similar observations were made earlier by McDowell (1984) based on the data obtained from a number of countries on the performance of the cross-bred animals.

Cross-bred cows are more profitable to maintain than indigenous cows. Probably because of this the farmers (in places where there is emphasis on cross-breeding) value cross-bred females much more than indigenous females. They also take more care and feed the cross-bred cows better. There are reports that the farmers in Operational Research Project (ORP) area of Karnal earned about Rs. 14 million through the sale of cross-bred animals (Singh, 1991). For this reason farmers like to possess and maintain cross-bred heifers and cows for sale rather than for milk production in Haryana. The reverse argument holds good for farmers of Karnataka and Maharashtra where organised remunerative market and increased demand for cow milk are available. The reasons attributed by George and Nair (1990) for the spectacular success achieved in implementing the cross-breeding programme in Kerala were growth in demand for milk, increased returns from milk production, decline in the requirements of work animals in agriculture and expansion of the market for beef.

All these field studies reviewed clearly indicated that cross-bred cows outdo the indigenous cows on various reproduction and milk production parameters. Though, there are no reports indicating the extent of contribution of cross-bred cows in total milk production, cross-breds must have contributed to some extent in increasing the milk production which is a desirable consequence. Vaidyanathan (1989) remarked that cross-breeding technology may contribute to increase in milk production, but it will be at the expense of draught power availability in the small and marginal farms and increased application of fossil fuel to the agricultural sector.

Researchers had attempted to compare the draught power of cross-bred bullocks with that of indigenous bullocks on various parameters such as draught power, speed output,

Table 2.3 : Comparison between Cross-bred and Indigenous Bullocks on Draught Capacity Parameters

Parameter	Cross-breds Superior	Cross-breds Inferior	No Difference
Draught Power	Anand and Sundaresan, 1974; Acharya *et al.*, 1979	Nagpaul *et al.* 1984; Upadhyay and Madan, 1985; Sreekumar and Thomas, 1990	Roy *et al.*, 1972; Bhosrekar and Mangurkur, 1989.
Ploughing Ability	Roy *et al.*, 1972	Sreekumar and Thomas, 1990	Rao *et al.*, 1974; Nagpaul *et al.*, 1984.
Heat Adaptability	—	Thomas and Pearson, 1986; Sreekumar and Thomas, 1990	
Draught Potential in Summer	—	Bhatnagar *et al.*, 1977; Upadhyay and Madan, 1985; Nagpaul, 1987	
Work Efficiency	Upadhyaya and Madan, 1985	Roy *et al.*, 1972; 1985; Sreekumar and Thomas, 1990	Nagpaul *et al.*, 1984
Draught Potential in Hot Humid Conditions	Sreekumar and Thomas, 1990	Roy *et al.*, 1972	

ploughing ability, physiological responses, work efficiency, feed conversion efficiency and their performance under different climatic conditions (Table 2.3).

The studies (Nagpaul *et al.*, 1984; Upadhyaya and Madan, 1985; Sreekumar and Thomas, 1990; Venkatasubramanian and Fulzele, 1996) were indicative of the hypothesis that cross-bred bullocks were inferior to indigenous bullocks in terms of draught power, ploughing ability and work efficiency. Cross-bred bullocks showed distress with increased loads and they had less heat adaptability than indigenous bullocks (Thomas and Pearson, 1985 and Sreekumar and Thomas, 1990). The indigenous animals were reported to be superior to cross-breds in their work efficiency and rate of recovery from stress caused by work. Similarly, cross-breds were observed to show distress symptoms on carrying increased loads (Nagpal *et al.*, 1984; Upadhyaya and Madan, 1985 and Bhosrekar and Mangurkar, 1989). With increased duration of work hours cross-breds showed more distress symptoms than indigenous bullocks (Acharya *et al.*, 1979; Gattewar, 1983; Bhosrekar and Mangurkar, 1989 and Sreekumar and Thomas, 1990). However, Acharya (1989) was of the view that most of the cross-breds especially halfbreds, performed better than the indigenous males because of their size.

Farmers were also of the view that cross-bred male calves not become good bullocks (Patel *et al.*, 1980). Probably, because of this feeling cross-bred male calves were neglected after birth resulting in their poor growth, pot belly condition, rough hair coat, and the majority of them were eliminated through natural death (Venkatasubramanian and Fulzele, 1996). George and Nair (1990) reported that all holdings surveyed in Kerala sold their male calves. This explains to some extent the reason behind fewer cross-bred male calves in less than one year and one to two-year categories. There is no denying the fact that cross-bred male was an unwanted calf but because of religious considerations the farmers, instead of culling it through slaughter, wait for its natural death or leave it in public places. The same thing holds good for the *desi* calves as well. In the process the country is losing a number of crossbred males without contributing anything to Indian economy (Rao *et al.,* 1995).

It is true that as a whole there is a decline in the draught animals. This may be because of the decline in the average size of land holding as was the case in Tamil Nadu (Dhas, 1989) and Kerala (Vaidyanathan, 1989) or to the increased intensity of agricultural mechanization in States like Punjab and Haryana.

Comparative studies on draught power clearly revealed that cross-bred bullock is no match for indigenous bullock in heat adaptability and draught potential in summer and hot humid climates. There were no definite indications on other parameters. As the cross-bred male is neglected right from the birth there may be less opportunity for the cross-bred bullock to prove their worth. The poor demand for cross-bred bullocks could be explained by the fact that they consume more water and are unable to bear heat stress. There were isolated cases where the farmers changed their system of ploughing by shifting to early morning and evening hours for utilizing the services of cross-bred bullocks, the price of which is very much lower than indigenous bullock pairs. Hence, evolution of cross-bred males as a sequel to the implementation of cross-breeding programme is a negative or undesirable consequence especially when viewed against the fact that bullock power continues to be the main stay for agricultural operations in the years to come (Rao *et al.*, 1995).

It is often argued that cross-bred animals are susceptible to diseases and hence need more care. Studies reflecting this feature under field conditions are scanty. On the basis of field data Venkatasubramanian and Rao (1991) concluded that cross-breds were more prone to diseases than indigenous cattle. The studies conducted on organised herds revealed that the incidence of gastro-intestinal disorders, FMD, Pox and eye problems were reported to be high in cross-breds as compared to Red Sindhi, Sahiwal and Tharparkar breeds (Singh *et al.*, 1986b). Sharma and Jain (1984) observed that cross-breds suffered higher prenatal calf losses than purebred zebu. The incidence of theileriosis was observed only in cross-breds and not a single case is reported either in indigenous cattle or buffaloes (Rao and Sohal, 1985; Venkatasubramanian and Rao, 1992). As a result the cross-bred cattle owners have to get their animals vaccinated against various diseases which include foot and mouth, rinder- pest, theileriosis etc., or get them treated if affected with the disease which is very expensive.

These reports confirm the fear that if proper steps are not taken, poor but resistant local cattle in due course of time will be replaced by disease prone cross-breds which is certainly an undesirable consequence. At the same time it is also possible to exploit the potentiality of cross-breds by providing proper health care and management.

It is argued that with the implementation of cross-breeding programme in India much of the indigenous germplasm is being lost. At this juncture it is apt to quote Hermitte (1989) who stated in unequivocal terms that "the pressure to provide the farmers with more productive breeds in third world countries could be harmful. It is indeed tempting to import cattle, transfer embryos into surrogate females, increase inseminations (which are not well supervised) and to carry out cross-breeding (that might erase the qualities of both breeds). The unfortunate result is that a poor but resistant type of livestock could be replaced within a few generations by a totally unadopted one. "He also remarked that cross-breeding as well as substitutions of certain breeds for others may mean destroying the local ones although they are still needed. Similar views were also expressed by Acharya (1989b) and Rao *et al.*, 1995. Cross-breeding, therefore, resulted in a negative genetic development of these indigenous breeds, which is certainly an undesirable consequence.

Cross-bred can produce more milk but they need more feed to exploit this potential. Pandey and Mishra (1985) estimated an average cost of feed of Rs. 2 for indigenous cows and Rs. 6.8 for cross-breds. This, however, depends heavily on the (variable) prices of the types of feeds. Cross-breds need more and better feed not only because they produce more milk but also due to their higher body weight which increases their maintenance requirements. Compared with a non-decrepit cow of 250 kg a cross-bred of 350 kg needs per day around 0.6 kg of TDN and 0.1 kg of CP more just to maintain its body functions which equals to about 1.2 to 1.6 kg of milk (based on NRC 1989) assuming equal maintenance requirements per kg. Cross-breds also need higher quality feeds because the intake of feed is not increased to the same magnitude as the increased requirements. The plus point for the native cattle is that they can eat and survive even on poor quality roughages while exotic breeds of cattle might lose weight or even starve (Orskovo, 1964).

The economic feasibility of feeding of high quality feeds like concentrates, depend upon their availability and prices in relation to output prices. As a rule of thumb, feeding of concentrates is beneficial if the prices of concentrates to milk are in the ratio lower than 1:1.25 assuming that 1 kg of concentrate is sufficient for producing 2 kg of milk, while roughages can meet the maintenance requirements. Because cross-breds have higher requirements for good quality feeds, and because they seem beneficial only if this ratio is lower than 1:1.25, assuming that little high quality fodders are available. In any case the demand for concentrate feed is bound to increase with increase in the female cross-bred population. With the increase in the total demand for milk products projects at 4.3 per cent per annum in the next two decades in India (Radhakrishnan, 1991) there will be an induced demand for feeds as well as fodders.

The cross-breeding programme could not create the desired impact on dairy development because of various constraints such as lack of clearcut breeding policy, implementation of cross-breeding programme irrespective of its applicability/ suitability to the area, lack of AI and veterinary aid facilities, repeat breeding and ban on slaughter of cattle in almost all the States. Even the provision of AI facilities does not guarantee the adoption of cross-breeding programme by the farmers as reported by Dhas (1991). McDowell (1984) opined that marginal to sub-marginal returns are a serious impediment to the adoption of breeding systems designed to increase genetic potential for milk yield. India is no exception to this contention that large AI programmes have been launched for cross-breeding without consideration of farmer priorities.

Summary

Cross-breeding technology helped in increasing the milk production though the extent of contribution of cross-breds to this is not clear and varies across India. Though the impact of cross-breeding programme on milk production is not as substantial as expected, there is no point in discontinuing it, rather it should be examined for its failure and success. It is unfortunate that much time and resources have been lost in the process of experimenting with cross-breeding in cattle to increase the genetic potential for milk production. It is high time for the planners and policy-makers to review the breeding policy and activities in the country with earnest consideration to the existing farming systems and farmer priorities.

The increased number of cross-breds induce an increased need for, especially high quality feeds, medicines and vaccines. Undesirable consequences of this cross-breeding technology are decrease in availability of draught animals. While in the process sturdy local cattle are getting replaced by comparatively more susceptible cross-breds, though at a slower pace.

Despite expending huge amounts of money on cross-breeding technology in addition to the supply of almost free of cost supply of semen to the farming community, this technology has shown its impact only in a few farming systems, probably mainly due to differences in conditions in farming systems. For successful implementation of this controversial cross-breeding technology it is necessary to ascertain before hand the conditions conducive for the technology. It is better to implement the cross-breeding programmes with vigour only in the potential promising areas rather than wasting resources in implementing the programme throughout the country. Important conditions influencing the successful implementation of cross-breeding include an increased demand for cow milk or young stock resulting in a remunerative market, low demand for draught animals, accessibility of veterinary assistance to farmers, and low prices of high quality feeds relative to milk prices.

References

Acharya, R.M (1989a). *Indian J. Anim. Sci.*, 59(2): 264-87.

Acharya, R.M. (1989b). In Gerald Weiner (Ed) : Animal Genetic Resources. A Global Programme for Sustainable Development, Proceedings of a FAO expert consultation September 1989, Rome, pp 197-206.

Acharya, S.M Mishra, and Nayak J.B. (1979). *Indian J Dairy Sci.* 32(1): 37-42.

Battacharya, P. (1984). Cattle and Buffalo Breeding : Past, Present and Future in Souvenir, NDRI, Karnal.

Bhatnagar, D.S.; Sharma, R.C. and Sundaresan, D (1977). Karan Swiss of NDRI, Karnal, NDRI Pub. No. 155.

Bhosrekar, M.R. and Mangurkar, B.R. (1989). *Indian J Dairy Sci.* 42(3): 612-13.

Cunningham, E.P. and Syrstad, O. (1987). Cross-breeding Bas Indices and Bas Taurus for Milk Production in the Tropics in FAO Animal Production and Health Paper, 68, pp 38-90, FAO, Rome.

Dhas, A.C. (1989). In *Livestock Economy of India,* Indian Society of Agricultural Economics, Oxford and IBH Publications, New Delhi.

Das, A.C. (1991). Structure of Milk Production in Tamil Nadu : An Analysis of Trends and Sources of Growth in Doornbos Martin and K.N. Nair, *Resources, Institutions and Strategies : Operation Flood and Indian Dairying*, Sage Publications, New Delhi.

Gattewar, A.B. (1983). *Working Capacity and Behaviour of Crossbred (F1) vs Zebu Cattle*, M.Sc. thesis, Haryana Agriculture University, Hissar.

George, P.S. and Nair, K.N. (1990). *Livestock Economy of Kerala*, Centre for Development Studies, Trivandrum, Kerala.

Government of India (1976). Report on National Commission on Agriculture. Vol. VII, Animal Husbandry, Ministry of Agriculture, New Delhi.

Hermitte, M.A (1989). In Gerald Werner (ed), *Animal Genetic Resources—A Global Programme for Sustainable Development*, Proceedings of an FAO expert consultation, Rome, pp. 13-26.

Jose, T.K. (1988). *XXII Dairy Industry Conference*, Trivandrum, pp 29-31.

Katpatal, B.G. (1977). *World Animal Review*, 23 : 2-9.

Kothavalla, Znl R. (1953). Proceedings of the 10th Meeting of Animal Husbandry Wing of the Board of Agriculture and Animal Husbandry in India, p 151.

McDowell, R.E. (1984). *J Dairy Sci.*, 68 : 2418-35.

Nagpaul, P.K.; Rao, M.V.N.; Singh C.B. and Bhatnagar, D.S. (1984). *World Rev. Anim. Prod*, 29(3) : 52-55.

Nair, K.N. (1979). *Economic and Political Weekly*, 24, pp A25-A39.

Orskov, Bob (1964). *New Scientist*, January 19.

Pandey, J.N. and Mishra, H.R.(1985). *Indian Dairyman*, 37 (6) : 243-47.

Patel, R.K.; Kumar, P.; Gangadharan, T.P.; Dhaka, J.P.; Voegele, K.; Srikumaran Nair, R. and Sreekumaran Nair G., (1976). Report of a Study of the Cattle Breeding Programme of Indo-Swiss Project, Kerala, NDRI, Karnal.

Patel, R.K.; Singh, C.B, Mahi Pal; Sarma, P.A.; Dass, S.C.; Shoi, D.S. and Dhaka, J.P. (1980). Report of Operational Research Project (1975-1981), NDRI, Karnal.

Prasad, V.S.; Narashimha Rao, G.; Satyanarayana, A.; Rama Rao, M. and Jayaramakrishna, V. (1991). *Indian J. Dairy Sci*, 44(2) : 194-95.

Radhakrishna, R. (1991). *Food and Nutrition 45th Annual Conference of Indian Society of Agricultural Statistics*, November.

Rao, K.R. (1981). Ph.D. thesis, Kurukshetra University, Kurukshetra.

Rao, M.V.N.; Raina, V.S.; Tomer, O.S.; Relwani, L.L. and Sharma K.N.S. (1974). Annual Report, NDRI, 1974.

Rao, S.V.N. and Sohal, T.S. (1985). Incidence and Treatment of Theileriosis in Crossbreds, *Dairy Guide*, 6(8) : 17-20.

Rao, S.V.N.; Venkatasubramanian, V. and Jan Dewit (1995). Consequences of Cross-Breeding Programme in India, *Economic and Political Weekly*. 30(39) : 112-116.

Rogers, E.M. (1983). *Diffusion of Innovations*, Free Press, New York.

Roy, S.R.; Neogi, A.K. and Guha, H. (1972). *Indian Dairyman*, 14 : 67-70.

Sahota, R.S. and Gill, G.S. (1990). *Livestock Adviser* 15(12) : 11-12.

Sharma, K.N.S. and Jain, D.K. (1984). *Indian J. Anim. Sci.* 54(4): 297-300.

Singh, Shivtar; Raul, K.C. and Jain, J.P. (1986a). *Indian J. Anim. Sci.*, 56 (5) : 542-45.

Singh, R.N.; Mishra, R.R; Dutta O.P.; Prabhakaran V.T. and Malhotra, J.C. (1986b). *Indian J. Anim. Sci.*, 56 (12) : 1229-33.

Singh, C.B. (1991). Programme and Achievements of Integrated Milk and Crop Production Project, Paper presented in Workshop-cum-Seminar held at NDRI, Karnal.

Singh, Jai Ram and Kulwant Singh (1991). *Dairy Guide* 13 (1-6):31-35.

Sreekumar, D. and Thomas, C.K. (1990). *Indian J Anim. Sci.*, 60(5):582-86.

Staempflif, H.; Valiathan Unnikrishnan, V.S. and Kuepfer, K. (1984). *Indian Dairyman*, 36:69.

Thomas, C.K. and Pearson, R.A. (1985). *Anim. Prod.* 43(1) : 83-90.

Upadhyaya, R.C. and Madan, M.L. (1985). *Indian J. Anim. Sci.* 55(1). 50-54.

Vaidyanathan, A. (1989). In *Livestock Economy of India, Indian Society of Agricultural Economics*, Oxford and IBH Publishing, New Delhi, pp. 1-43.

Van Duc Nguyen and Taneja, V.K. (1984). *Indian J. Anim. Sci.* 54(2): 141-44.

Venkatasubramanian, V. and Rao, S.V.N. (1992). *Indian J. Dairy Sci.* 46(7): 302-06.

Venkatasubramanian, V. and Fulzele, R.M. (1996). *Dairy Farming in Tropics*, MD Publishers, New Delhi.

3

STRENGTHS, WEAKNESSES, OPPORTUNITIES AND THREATS (SWOT) OF DAIRY DEVELOPMENT

Introduction

In the management sciences, SWOT analysis plays a paramount role in understanding the management problems at all stages irrespective of the type of organization and programmes. Until recently, the subject of SWOT analysis had been taught in the management studies and the concept is meant to help in taking appropriate decisions for the development of an organization or programme in a particular operational environment. The Leonard *et al.* (1993) has applied the SWOT concept on performance audit and contingent planning involving the development of specific action when lower probability events occurred. However, it was surmised that only those lower probability events would have important consequences for the organization. Cook (1994) applied SWOT analysis for strategic planning. He also developed simple worksheets systematically to arrive at the pros and cons for taking appropriate decision for any type of development programmes or organization to overcome hurdles.

Kothai (1993) has employed SWOT analysis on three development projects, viz., Farm Clinic, Sri Kshetra Dharmastala Rural Employment Project (SKDREP) and Integrated Rural Development Project (IRDP) and indicated its importance for consolidation of strengths for harnessing the available potentials further. Venkateswarlu and Kalla (1996) has applied the

SWOT concept in analyzing the National Agricultural Research Project (NARP) and discussed the strengths, weaknesses, opportunities and threats associated with the programme. Venkatasubramanian and Bandyopadhyay (1998) has analysed the strengths, weaknesses, opportunities and threats of Agricultural Development in Andaman and Nicobar Islands. The analysis has helped the islands authorities to consolidate the strengths, harness the scarce resources, remove the weaknesses, to formulate suitable strategies for combating the threats and to utilise the available opportunities for the development of agriculture in the remote islands. Economic analysis of strengths, weaknesses, opportunities and threats (SWOT) and its application in the field of agriculture is unlimited and therefore an attempt is made to analyse the dairy development programme by applying the SWOT concept.

Successful dairy development requires the ability and capacity on the part of planners to make correct decisions. To improve the management of resources and to achieve the desired level of success in the dairy development process, the dimensions such as formulating goals or objectives for development, recognising the problem and opportunity for development, obtaining of information about possible threats by constraints, specifying and analyzing the alternatives, successful implementation and evaluation of the programme are more important and plays the decisive role. Lack of relevant materials or information about the development potentials, opportunity for diversification, systems inability to understand the developmental process and possible alternatives for development severely constraints the decision making process. Therefore, the relevant information about strengths, weaknesses, opportunities and threats that are associated with the dairy development system in the country are of paramount importance.

Strengths refer to the basic assets or potentials of a thing that would provide competitive advantage for its growth and development. Weaknesses are the liabilities that can create a state of time and situation which acts on a specific disadvantage for its growth and development. Opportunities means the ability to grow and achieve the given specific objectives in a given direction and situation. Threats are the situations that block the abilities to grow, develop and progress in a given situation or environment. In this chapter the SWOT analysis concept has been applied in the context of dairy development in the country. The analysis helps to create a congenial environment and scientific base for discussing and taking crucial decisions with regard to dairy development in the islands. As it gives the foresight and considerable evidence of pros and cons, the probability of lateral stage failures is bound to be considerably reduced.

SWOT Analysis on Dairy Development

If we critically examine the programme evolution aspects of the white revolution in the country, it is evident that the objectives and strategies followed time to time has suffered with major weaknesses and inconsistencies. One of the major lacunae is the relative neglect of buffaloes and the failure to exercise the control over the implementation of breeding policy evolved which has led to the creation of crossbred cows with varying inheritance level and performance. Even though at the initial stage the policy was emphasizing the need to improve the milch cattle and draught cattle, in the event of introduction of cross-breeding programme through exotic breeds, the relative improvement of draught animals could not happen. It is in the latter half, the realisation of improvement and conservation of indigenous draught animals gained momentum and the efforts have been reinitiated. Therefore, neglecting the male stock in the event of improving the milk production is the clear deviation from the earlier line of thinking to evolve better dual purpose breeds as per the policy of KVS programme.

The earlier policy of evolving dual purpose breeds have taken the diversion because of the fault that majority of the animal husbandry experts and policy makers favoured the adoption of cross-breeding programme by crossing the indigenous breeds of cattle with exotic breeds like Jersey, Brown Swiss and Holstein-Friesien to achieve a quick breakthrough in the milk production. This shift in policy has been strengthened by the launch of ICDP and operation flood programmes. Some of the advantages gained due to the policy shift were the improved production and reproduction potentials of our cattle as the cross-bred cows have a lower age at first calving, longer lactation length, shorter inter-*calving* interval and higher milk yield per lactation. When the superiority of the cross-bred cows to its indigenous counterpart as milk animal is beyond doubt, it has its weaknesses in terms of poor draught power of the cross-bred male, susceptible to diseases and more nutritional requirements. The failure to eliminate the diseased and low productivity animals through slaughter has resulted in the increase of unproductive stock giving competition to the scarce fodder resources and emerged as a serious threat for future years. The higher disease susceptibility, calf mortality rate, declining of draught animal population and higher cost involved towards the maintenance of cross-bred cattle are some of the potential threats to be taken care of. Unless it is done the opportunity that dairying for rural change is under threat. Dairying as an instrument for helping the resources poor has by and large suffered from these operational difficulties that the relatively weaker sections and resource poor farmers need to struggle for the resources needed to maintain the high quality milch animals. So, the dairying as an opportunity to achieve the rural development has by and large need to be maintained and it should not be confined to the relatively resourceful sections in rural areas than the resource poor sections. It is against this background an attempt has been made in this section to understand the extent to which the strengths, weaknesses, opportunities and threats associated with our dairy development over the years in actuality has influenced the performance of our dairy sector and its implication over its performance in the future.

Strengths

The features that can be considered as potential strengths that favour the dairy development of the country are listed and discussed in this section. The heterogeneous and well diversified farming locations, greater diversity and availability of potential resources favours a sustainable dairy farming even at the small farmers level. By and large the agricultural farming in the country is less mechanised and, therefore, the agriculture has to depend on the livestock for the farm energy requirements. Therefore, a normal Indian farmer has to keep the livestock for his farm operations and dairying as a small scale farm enterprise always exists in the rural household. This aspects of Indian dairying is popularly known as milk production by masses and it differs from the concept of mass production of milk followed in the developed countries. The above aspects of our dairy sector is, therefore, the basic strength of our dairy development as it assures the livelihood for millions of farm families in the rural India.

Strengths of Dairy Development

- Heterogeneous and well diversified farming locations
- Less mechanised agricultural farming
- High demand for milk and milk products
- Sound research and technological support
- Infrastructure in terms of physical and man-power resources
- Establishment of three-tier Anand type of co-operatives and farmers participation
- Urban-Rural linkage and national milk grid
- Rural upliftment towards self-reliance
- Significant contribution to national income, foreign exchange revenue and consultancy aspects
- World leader in milk production
- Strong industrial base and support
- Genetically upgraded indigenous cattle
- Presence of strong buffalo base
- Development of indigenous milk breeds
- Protection of both producer and consumer interest

Even though, the country has achieved remarkable strides in the milk production, still there exists a huge gap between the demand and supply. In the true sense, there is no marketable surplus of milk with the majority of milk producing small farm families if they consume the milk to meet their nutritional requirement. It is the mandatory requirement for the country to meet the minimum nutritional level of the people and to achieve the real pace of development, the per capita availability of the milk, therefore, at least should be raised to the minimum standard prescribed by WHO. Therefore, there exists a huge opportunity to further increase the milk production in the country to assure food security to the masses. The demand for milk and milk products in the country is forever due to its huge population size. The country has established a number of research establishments at national and regional levels to support the dairy development programme.

The State Agricultural Universities, National Dairy Development Board and Indian Council of Agricultural Research through research institutes and laboratories have developed their number of technologies to improve the milk production in the country. They have helped to indigenise the milk production and processing technologies. A number of break-throughs have been achieved in the fields of dairy cattle genetics and breeding, health care, nutrition, biotechnology, embryo transfer and milk processing.

The infrastructural development required for the dairy development during the ICDP and operation flood programme is commendable. During the initial plan period, the facilities required for upgradation of the cattle, health care facilities and conducting research have been taken care of. A total financial grant amount of Rs. 12,941 million has been spent towards the establishment of infrastructural facilities during the Operation Flood Programme. This excludes the amount spent on regular plan and non-plan amount allocated for dairying. The establishment of 26 State Agricultural Universities, Veterinary Colleges, Dairy Technology Institutes, Veterinary

Universities and Rural Management Institutes are some of the standing examples of country's strength towards the human resource development required for dairy development. The establishment of National Dairy Development Board with functional autonomy to look after the dairy development in the country is the standing example for the development initiative taken up by the Government of India.

During 1970-71, the number of milk co-operatives in the country were 1,588 with 2,78,000 producers and an annual milk procurement level of 0.1898 million tonnes. At the end of 1981 the number of milk co-operatives increased to 13,270, with a member producers of 17,47,000 and 0.9844 million tonnes annual milk procurement. During 1990 at the end of Operation Flood-III, the country was having 60,825 village level milk producers co-operative societies, comprising of 7,003,000 member farmers with an annual milk procurement level of 3.5821 million tonnes. No doubt it is a commendable achievement which ensured the farmers participation in the programme and assured back them the return.

The urban-rural linkage achieved as a result of the Operation Flood Programme is yet another model to simulate in the third world. In countrics like Australia, New Zealand, Denmark, U.S.A., Canada and U.K., the dairy sector operates on large scale and the operational holding is largely concentrated and pooled. In our country, the situation is reverse wherein the milk production by masses and operational holding is small and scattered. The milk producing centres are located away from the demand centres. There was uneven production and supply of milk. Such situations have put both producers and consumers in very great distress. The establishment of national milk grid has facilitated the movement of milk from surplus centres to demand centres and ensured a steady procurement, supply and price throughout the country. This has helped to ensure the producers and consumers their price.

Due to its strength of assuring a steady income to the rural households, the dairying has been viewed as a tool or mode for poverty alleviation and it has become a part of rural development programmes currently in operation. This has increased the participation level and in turn helps to increase our milk production. The presence of strong buffalo base, and cross-breds have ensured the returns to rural producers and helped to achieve self-reliance in the rural economy.

Weaknesses

The dairy development policy over the years have undergone dramatic changes and suffered from inconsistencies. One of the major lacunae is its relative failure to recognise and promote buffalo as a milch animal. If we compare with the time and energy spent in cross-breeding of our cattle, very little has been done to promote the buffalo.

Even though the cross-breeding technology helped in increasing the milk production, the extent of its contribution is not clear and varies across India. Though the impact of cross-breeding programme on milk production is not substantial, no serious efforts have been taken till date to review the situation for correcting its failure.

The question of weaknesses will come into limelight when the principle components of dairying such as breeding, feeding, slaughter, issues of rural change etc. are analysed critically.

Initially there existed a general emphasis on the need to improve the quality of milk cattle and draught animals simultaneously. Similarly, equal emphasis was given in the development of buffalo and it was recognised as the potential milch animal under Indian conditions. With this understanding only the KVS was initiated during the first Plan period. In middle of sixties, however, the policy has taken a dramatic shift in favour of cross-breeding programme. The shift has resulted in the launching of ICDP and has been further intensified in the Operation Flood Projects. This approach of cross- breeding has also been recognised and received encouragement from the National Commission on Agriculture.

Cross-breeding programme has generated lot of controversy since its inception. The literature is full of arguments in favour and against the implementation of this sensitive programme. With the involvement of various agencies in the cross-breeding programme, it is often reported that the services are duplicated and many times the achievements are claimed by more than one agency. Moreover, cross-breeding programme could not be able to create the desired impact due to the presence of various constraints. Few States like Uttar Pradesh, Kerala, Tamil Nadu, West Bengal and Maharashtra accounted for about 80 per cent of the total cross-bred population of the country. To analyse the consequences of this programme an in-depth study was conducted by Venkatasubramanian and Fulzele, 1996 covering different farming locations representing the coastal, plain and hilly conditions and the salient findings of the study are summarized here:

1. The conspicuous absence of cross-bred bullocks and considerable reduction of indigenous bullocks among the farmers implied that draught animal power is continuously decreasing. Therefore, steps must be taken to improve the declining draught animal power and preservation of some of the excellent indigenous draught breeds such as Kangayam, Umbalachery, Hallikar, Amirtmahal, Haryana etc.
2. There was less variation in the performance of cross-breds and indigenous cattle with respect to the size of the land holding. Within the breed variation in the performance was noticed with respect to the level of various management practices followed by the farmers. The small and medium farmers were actively involved in the dairy enterprise to supplement their agricultural income. This suggested that it was the farmers' interest and their level of entrepreneurship shown towards dairying, has influenced the performance of cross-breds in their farm than their size of

agricultural operation. Successful implementation of various dairy development programmes catering to the needs of small, medium and landless category is warranted. Moreover, providing other input services like easy availability of loans, health coverage and marketing facilities will further help dairy farmers to be more enterprising.

3. The regional and agro-climatic zonewise variations in the performance of the cross-breds were seen. Apart from the genetic variations, the variation in the farming system along with environmental differences caused much variations. Therefore, suitable on-farm experiments need to be carried out in determining the breed suitability, the optimum level of the exotic germplasm and the extent of coverage through cross-breeding programme with respect to farming systems and climatic conditions.
4. The perception by farmers that cross-bred bullocks are no more a draught animal and the discrimination shown to cross-bred males are suggestive of the fact that almost all the cross-bred males born were of no use to the farmer. Suitable on-farm trials can be conducted to determine the speed output, work suitability, adaptability to thermal stress and other draught parameters of cross-breds in comparison with their indigenous counterparts under different climatic conditions and farming system locations to make concrete suggestions to the farmers for making optimum use of their cross-bred bullocks.
5. The incidence of various health disorders in crossbreds were higher than the indigenous cattle. In the farms where suitable health care measures have been taken, the incidences of health disorders were less. The high incidence of digestive disorders in both the cross-breds and indigenous cattle suggested that often the farmers were feeding their stock with poor quality feeds and fodder. The feeding management

in the farm was greatly influenced by the availability of feeds and fodder which showed a high areawise variation.

The incidence of theileriosis was completely absent in indigenous cattle and buffalo whereas the cross-breds were very often suffered with the ailment. Therefore, it is suggested that along with the exotic level of germ-plasm optimum level of disease resistant indigenous germplasm should be maintained. Through extension contact and suitable bio-conversion techniques, good quality of feeds and fodder can be made available to the farmers by enriching the nutrient content of local feeds and fodder.

6. The programme was constrained by farmers frequent missing of heat in their animals, high rate of repeat breeding problem, distant location of AI centres in some areas, improper handling of semen before and during insemination, high cost of concentrates, poor quality of fodder and inadequate availability of greens, farmers ignorance about balanced feeding, inadequate supply of medicines, problems of quacks, inadequate infrastructural facilities, lack of recognition for good work, lack of co-ordination and co-operation between various agencies, unrealistic targets and poor communication facilities available with dairy development workers, presence of scrub bulls, socio-cultural and religious taboos prevailing among the people. Suitable remedial measures need to be taken to remove the above weaknesses for giving better impetus to the dairy development.

The other important weaknesses were the presence of large unproductive cattle, failure of the dairy co-operatives to evoke equal level of success in all the States. The reasons for such performance differences among the milk co-operatives have been studied in detail and discussed in chapter five.

It was pointed out that higher economic motivation, commitment level, higher milk sale by members, less politicised environment, absence of groupism/caste politics, and loyalty to the society contributed to the successful performance of the society. The presence of groupism/casteism, disloyalty of member farmers, sabotaging activities of the local milk vendors/private dairy operators, low efficiency level of the office bearers, lower milk collection rate and farmers' direct accessibility to urban marketing centre are some of the reasons for failure of the milk co-operatives.

Lack of proper monitoring, controlling and evaluation at various levels at timely intervals failed to review the progress and give appropriate feedback are some of the important contributing factors for the failure of milk co-operatives. In addition to this the concept of milk co-operatives has been extended indiscriminately on the basis of its initial success in few States. In choosing the project areas the implementing agencies need to acertain the suitability of the areas on the basis of project objectives and resources. There is no information on the economic and social cost-benefit of these projects. Consequences in terms of output, employment, consumption, savings, income distribution and other tangible benefits are to be estimated. The consequences brought out must be evaluated from all the dimensions including the social aspects which is essential for making sound development policy. The impact of the dairy co-operatives on the adoption of innovations by the farmers have been studied by a number of researchers (Rao, 1975; Mikkilienin, 1976: Nachiappan and Srinivasamurthy, 1976; Puthusamy, 1976; Sidhu, 1980; Patel, 1980; Subramanian, 1982 and Venkatasubramanian, 1994). Other studies have concentrated in assessing extension performance by measuring the extent of farmers-dairy development agency interactions. Few studies like Venkatasubramanian, 1994 have examined the role of various agencies and their relative performance with respect to dairy development.

Presently the milk is being processed in the dairies

functioning under government, private and co-operative sectors. It is stated that not more than 20 per cent of the milk is being handled by this organised sector. The private dairies are mostly involved in the manufacture of milk products with little or no attention to the supply of fluid milk to the consumers. Wherever the private dairies are existing the public sector and co-operative dairies are facing stiff competition in milk procurement as well as sale of milk products. Incidentally, the private dairies are concentrated in the north-western part of the country. With the recent liberalization policy of the government many more dairies are entering into the market. These private dairies are concentrating on collecting buffalo milk which is required for manufacturing the products. Very little attention is paid by them to increase the milk production or educate the farmers in clean milk production resulting in huge losses due to spoilages.

The absence of regular and remunerative market for milk and milk products is a major constraint encountered by the farmers (Patel, *et al.,* 1978; Rao and Sastri, 1984; Rao, 1987; Sharma and Makhija, 1991; and Venkatasubramanian and Ramachand, 1991). Lack of inadequate credit facilities to the farmers for dairy purpose and exploitation by the middle men hampers the farmers from deriving maximum profit from dairying (Acharya, 1984; Gupta and Dipak De, 1989; Nayak *et al.*, 1986; Sharma,1980; and Venkatasubramanian and Fulzele, 1996).

Opportunities

At present the dairy development activities are being carried out by national level organisations such as NDDB, ICAR and its Institutes and State level organisations like milk federations, animal husbandry departments and non-government organisations. The success of these organisations in achieving the objectives rest with their ability to harness the available opportunities in the best possible way to bring about the desirable change process or improvement in the coming years.

Weaknesses of Dairy Development

— Inconsistency in Livestock Development policy and conflicting goals.
— Negative consequences of cross-breeding programme.
— Failure to promote buffalo.
— Wide mandate and duplication of services.
— Socio-cultural inhibitions.
— Presence of large unproductive cattle and buffalo population.
— Failure of dairy co-operatives to evoke success in all States.
— Small and scattered herds.
— Low per capita availability of milk.
— Underutilised infrastructure.
— Unequal distribution of dairy industries.
— Inadequate credit facilities.
— Variation in demand and supply.
— Private milk marketing system.
— Competition over dairy products and poor marketing strategy by co-operatives.
— Lack of professionalism.
— Lack of co-ordination and co-operation among the agencies involved in dairy development.
— Lack of proper monitoring, controlling and evaluation of the programmes.
— Inadequate grassroots level extension system.
— Politicisation of Dairy Co-operatives.
— Lack of proper surveillance and disease reporting system.
— Huge cost involved in Animal Health Care.
— Lack of trained technical manpower at the grass-roots level.
— Social taboos and religious beliefs.
— Inadequate participation of NGO and R&D organisations.

Opportunities of Dairy Development

- Promotion of buffaloes as milch animals.
- Evolving of clear cut National Policy.
- Eliminating the unproductive cattle.
- Strengthening of co-operative structures.
- Milk Production by masses.
- Less external input and sustainable dairying.
- Promotion of farming system approach.
- Fodder development and identification of alternative feed sources.
- Embryo transfer technology and in-vitro fertilisation technique.
- Tapping of non-conventional fodder resources.
- Strengthening of grassroots level structures.
- Tapping of export market potentials.
- Improvement of the health care facilities.
- Defining a clear cut breeding policy.
- Disease resistant indigenous cattle and buffaloes.
- Draught potential of our indigenous cattle.
- Development of potential areas/States suitable for dairying.
- Elimination of disparity among the milk production system.
- Protection of weaker section and promotion of dairying among them as a tool for poverty alleviation and self-reliance.
- Empowerment of women.
- Utilisation of Indigenous Technical Knowledge (ITK).
- Promoting co-ordination and co-operation among the development agencies.
- Self-generation of resources and elimination of foreign aid.
- Diversification of research and development programmes related to dairying.

Threats of Dairy Development

— Competition and entry of multi-nationals.
— High cost of concentrates and lack of adequate fodder resources.
— Huge cattle population and its competition over scarce resources.
— Scrub bulls and cross-bred males.
— Disease susceptibility of cross-breds.
— High cost of maintenance of cross-bred cattle.
— Increased cost of milk production.
— Urban-rural divide.
— Existence of unorganised milk marketing system.
— Lack of remunerative price for milk.
— Lack of credit availability to farmers and exploitation by money lenders.
— Exploitation by middle men and traders.
— High operational cost of dairy industries and underutilized plant capacity.
— Unforeseen and negative consequences of cross-breeding programme.
— Duplicacy of research and uneven development priorities.
— Non-implementation of stringent quality control measures in liquid milk marketing.
— Lack of commitment among dairy development personnel.
— Poor grassroots level functionaries.
— Organisational problems.
— Prevalence of wide gap and variation in the technology adoption process.

All along the buffaloes are neglected and their potential as milch animal still need to be exploited. Our policy should take into account the environment under which animals have to live and produce. Unless considerable improvement is made in the environment of the stock it is difficult to get the possible outcome from the cross-breds. The buffaloes are more capable to adopt to the prevailing farming situation and match the production performance at par with the cross-breds. Under the existing resources of Indian farmers, it is difficult to maintain separate breed of animals for milk and draught purposes. In most parts of the country, farmers are using buffaloes as draught animals also. The resource sustainability at small farmer level need to be protected for ensuring a long term survival of this sector.

As pointed out in the earlier sections, the dairy development policy needs consistency and a clear cut national policy which needs to be worked out and implemented. In the present situation, there is no definite programme with respect to the cattle development and results of the earlier efforts made could not be able to evoke the expected impact uniformly across the country. The major part of our efforts are wasted due to the presence of unproductive stock which also compete with the meagre feed resources. As a solution to this problem and an alternative to slaughter these stocks can be shipped to the forests and shall be left wild. This will considerably relieve the stress of agricultural resources such as land, water and which are otherwise overburdened. The shrinking wild cattle population in our forest can be improved by injecting these stock and in due course of time over natural selection a new breed can also be evolved.

There is no doubt that the milch co-operatives started in different parts of the country has brought forth the participation of rural producers and secured them from the clutches of traders but it has also made to realise the rural milk producers that the success and failure of the system lies in their hands only. The milk co-operatives though expected to evoke a uniform success story throughout the country, due to the prevailing socio-economic, cultural and political differences among the States, it could not be able to perform uniformly in all the States. In States like Haryana, Punjab, U.P. and North Eastern parts of the country, the co-operative structures have yielded to the local politics and become defunct. Therefore, a serious thought is to be given to find out where the fault is and corrective measures need to be carried out in the structure/function accordingly so that the desirable impact can be brought out in these States also for benefiting the real producers.

India being the country with lot of diversified farming locations and dairying being practiced by the masses rather than mass production. Dairying is, therefore, largely viewed as an important tool for the poverty alleviation bringing self-reliance to the rural poor and farmers. Agriculture in this country even though practiced as main occupation, due to its dependence on monsoon and uncertain price for the produce the farmers are bound to depend on animal husbandry as a source of security (to maintain sustenance) and additional income. Therefore, the small size cattle herd need to be encouraged rather than encouraging large size dairy sector simulating the western countries where the mass production of milk is practiced.

Due to the introduction of cross-breeding programme, the farmers are forced to depend more on external inputs and resources. Previously, the breeding bull was at his door steps whereas now he has to largely depend on AI centres and private practitioners for the breeding purposes. Similarly, the improved management practices required for these animals made him to rely upon more on the external resources than his own system. Therefore, it is the need of the hour to promote the technologies in such a way that enough internal resources are created within the system so that farmers can opt for these new technologies without any long term dependence upon the external resources. Similarly, the opportunities such as promotion of fodder production system, and exploration of suitable non-conventional feed resources, are to be made.

By promoting suitable disease surveillance measures, strict monitoring and restriction of cattle movement, the spread of cattle epidemics can be controlled. More serious efforts are to be made with respect to disease prevention and control than the sporadic attempts during the outbreaks alone. With regard to the national programmes on Rinderpest, FMD and Protozoan diseases, still there are opportunities to cover the endemic areas more systematically and uniformly. In addition, a thorough field level study over the cattle epidemics, the size of the preventive measures undertaken and its impact need to be carried out for formulating a perspective plan for the future.

Threats

Threats are the situations that hinder the abilities to grow, develop and progress in a given environment. The recent liberalisation policy has paved the ways for the multi-national entry in this sector which in turn threatens the indigenous dairy sector. Some may argue that such fear over the liberalisation issue is unwarranted and the entry of multi-national will no way harm the Indian dairy industry. Entry of NDDB to organise the Sri Lankan Dairy Industry in line with that of Anand pattern and its subsequent failure due to the organised efforts of multi-nationals is a standing example before us to take every step for protecting our dairy industry from the multi-nationals. Any such politically driven policy of allowing the field open to multi-nationals will certainly negate the progress in this field which lies in the hands of millions of dairy farmers in the country.

Growing demand for the grains and high cost of concentrates prohibits the farmers from providing the required nutritional feed to their cattle. The cross-breeding programme has led to the requirement of compulsory feeding with high quality feed and rich plan of nutrition failuring which the performance of cross-breeds comes nearer to the indigenous cattle. Efforts are, therefore, need to be made towards the solving of above problem for ensuring the sustainability to Indian Dairying.

Huge cattle population and its competition is one of the prime and potential threats need to be taken care of for the future survival. Our culture and religious sanctions prohibits slaughtering or any other means of culling the unproductive cattle. Often the issue is politicised. As a result more than 50 per cent of the stock are of no use except consuming the scarce fodder resources. Here is the situation which needs a policy intervention from the government to eliminate the unproductive stock from the scenario to save the precise resources of the country. As an alternative, these stock can be let off at the nearby jungles or reserve forests. Such measure will eliminate the scrub bulls which are mainly responsible for the contamination of high grade cross-breds with inferior germplasm.

The disease susceptibility of the cross-breds is yet another potential threat which needs immediate redressal. The results of the field study conducted by Venkatasubramanian and Fulzele, 1996 with respect to the disease incidence in the cross-bred and indigenous cattle are discussed hereunder for a proper understanding.

Incidences of Health Disorders

The results of incidence of various health disorders in cross-breds and indigenous cattle are presented in Table 3.1. From this table it is evident that about 37 per cent of the total cross-bred animals were affected with one or the other ailments, whereas for indigenous cattle the corresponding figure was 21 per cent. This indicated the superiority of indigenous cattle over cross-breds with respect to their disease resistance capacity. A similar finding was reported by Venkatasubramanian and Rao (1993). Out of the total 1185 animals affected by various ailments, about 72.80 per cent of the animals were cross-breds. The information on the type of health disorders to which the animals were affected can be had from the Table 3.2. Digestive disturbances accounted for a majority 31 per cent of the total cases recorded in white cattle. There was a difference between crossbreds and indigenous cattle with respect to digestive disorders. These findings were in conformity with that of

Table 3.1. Incidence of Health Disorders in Cross-bred and Indigenous Cattle in the Study Area

	Cross-bred	Indigenous	Total
Number of animals affected with ailments	863 (72.83)	322 (27.17)	1185 (100.00)
Total Population	2344 (60.95)	1502 (39.05)	3846 (100.00)
Percentage of animals affected with ailments	36.81	21.43	

Note : Figures in parentheses are percentage to total.

Singh *et al.* (1986) and contrary to that of Venkatasubramanian and Rao (1993) who reported that not much difference was discernible among cross-breds and indigenous cattle with respect to the incidence of digestive disorders.

Next in the order of importance were general ailments such as fever, skin infections, eye and ear infections which accounted for about 29 per cent of the total cases recorded. Here also the incidence was higher in cross-breds than in

Table 3.2. Incidence of Various Types of Health Disorders in Cross-breds and Indigenous Cattle

Nature of Disorders	Cross-bred	Indigenous	Total
Digestive	286 (33.14)	82 (25.46)	368 (31.05)
General	254 (29.43)	85 (26.39)	339 (28.60)
Reproductive	164 (19.00)	55 (17.08)	219 (18.48)
Parasitic	98 (11.35)	58 (18.01)	156 (13.16)
Respiratory	29 (3.36)	24 (7.45)	53 (4.47)
Mammary Gland	32 (3.70)	18 (5.59)	50 (4.21)
Total	863 (100.00)	322 (100.00)	1185 (100.00)

Note : Figures in parentheses are percentage to total.

the indigenous cattle. These findings were contrary to those of Singh *et al.* (1987) and Venkatasubramanian and Rao (1993) who reported that the incidence of fever, eye problems and other miscellaneous ailments were more in indigenous cattle than in cross-breds under field conditions. It was also evident from the same table that reproductive disorders were slightly more in cross-breds (19 per cent) compared to indigenous cattle (17.08 per cent). Singh *et al.* (1987), Sharma and Jain (1984) and Venkatasubramanian and Rao (1993) also observed similar finding. On the whole, 16.48 per cent of the white cattle were found to be suffering from one or the other reproductive ailment.

The percentage of animals affected with parasitic disorders was 13.16 with indigenous cattle reporting higher incidence (18 per cent) compared to the cross-breds (11 per cent). This was mainly due to the extra care the farmers were taking in deworming the cross-bred calves than the indigenous calves. Moreover, the work bullocks were often taken to community water tank which acted as a constant source of parasitic infection. The above findings contradicted the results of Venkatasubramanian and Rao (1993) who reported that there was no marked difference between cross-breds and indigenous cattle in the incidence of parasitic disorder.

The incidence of respiratory and mammary gland disorders were low with only about four per cent of the animals reported to have been affected with these disorders. A high incidence of respiratory disorders among indigenous cattle (7.45 per cent) was noticed because of their increased incidence of occurrence in work cattle which were mostly affected by the dust and stress during rigorous agricultural work.

In order to get a detailed understanding of various problems under each of the six categories of disorders the information was presented and discussed under each category separately.

Digestive Disorders

Among the various types of digestive disorders, anorexia accounted for 29 per cent in cross-breds and 32 per cent in case of the indigenous cattle (Table 3.3). Next in the order of importance were indigestion, gastro-enteritis and diarrhoea. The incidence of anorexia, enteritis, diarrhoea and tympany were comparatively low in cross-breds. A high incidence of indigestion (25.52 per cent) was seen in the cross-breds while it was 12.19 per cent in case of indigenous cattle. In general, the incidence of digestive disorders in the cattle was attributed to the prevailing feeding practices in the study area. Due to the variation in the availability of green fodder, exorbitant prices of concentrates, many farmers were forced to feed more of roughage mainly paddy straw and very little concentrates to their animals which might be causing the digestive disturbances.

Table 3.3. Incidence of Digestive Disorders in Cross-breds and Indigenous Cattle

Digestive disorders	Cross-breds	Indigenous
Anorexia	85 (29.72)	27 (32.92)
Indigestion	73 (25.52)	10 (12.19)
Gastro-enteritis	42 (14.68)	19 (23.17)
Diarrhoea	26 (9.09)	7 (8.54)
Impaction	25 (8.79)	11 (13.42)
Tympany	20 (6.99)	6 (7.31)
Calf scours	15 (5.24)	2 (2.43)
Total	286 (100.00)	82 (100.00)

Note : Figures in parentheses are percentage to total.

General Disorders

The general disorders include fever, dermatitis, milk fever, joint ill, etc. Among these disorders, fever and pyrexia ranked first with an incidence of as high as 44 per cent in cross-breds and 31 per cent in indigenous cattle (Table 3.4). About 16 per cent of the indigenous cattle were treated for dermatitis whereas the incidence was comparatively low (12.99 per cent) in cross-breds. This was mainly due to the rigorous work done in the field by the indigenous bullocks and indiscriminate practice followed by the farmers in the calf rearing practices as most of the reported dermatitis cases were seen in indigenous calves only. Cross-breds being

Table 3.4. Incidence of Various General Disorders in Cross-breds and Indigenous Cattle

Sl. No.	Type of disorders	Cross-breds	Indigenous
1.	Fever/Pyrexia	113 (44.48)	27 (31.76)
2.	Dermatitis	33 (12.99)	14 (16.47)
3.	Milk fever	44 (17.32)	—
4.	Navel ill/joint ill	42 (16.53)	11 (12.94)
5.	Eye/ear infection	16 (6.23)	8 (9.41)
6.	Epimeral fever	2 (0.78)	3 (3.52)
7.	Horn injuries	1 (0.39)	3 (3.52)
8.	Hoof injuries	—	4 (4.70)
9.	Avitaminosis	3 (1.18)	2 (2.35)
10.	Debility	—	13 (15.29)
	Total	254 (100.00)	85 (100.00)

Note : Figures in parentheses are percentage to total.

comparatively high yielders, the incidence of milk fever were 17 per cent, whereas not even a single case was found among the indigenous cattle. A similar finding was reported by Venkatasubramanian and Rao (1993). The incidence of eye and ear infection, horn and hoof injuries were high in indigenous cattle because most of them were associated with the work related injuries in indigenous bullocks during their heavy work in the field. There were 15 per cent of the debility cases reported in indigenous cattle whereas none in the cross-breds. This showed the farmers' negligence in feeding the indigenous cattle considering them as poor milkers. On the contrary, they were observed to be taking greater care in the management of cross-breds. Moreover, the high price of cross-bred cattle coupled with their high market demand influenced the farmers to provide better care and management to cross-breds whereas the indigenous cattle have been neglected. So, the farmers left some of their aged indigenous cattle with inadequate care and attention. The incidence of other ailments, such as avitaminosis and epimeral fever was very low.

Reproductive Disorders

From Table 3.5, it is evident that among the reproductive disorders, repeat breeding incidence was high both in the cross-breds (41.46 per cent) and indigenous cattle (38.18 per cent). This high percentage was mainly because of poor conception through AI which might be due to several reasons such as poor quality of semen, poor skills of the inseminators and farmers' inability to present the animals at proper time for AI. A similar finding was reported by Venkatasubramanian and Rao (1993).

Anoestrum was found to be the second most serious problem among cross-breds (20.73 per cent) as well as indigenous (18.18 per cent) animals. This was because of the low plan of nutrition in animals and mineral deficiencies. The animals were being maintained on dry fodder and a little

Table 3.5. Incidence of Reproductive Disorders in Cross-breds and Indigenous Cattle

Sl. No.	Type of Reproductive Disorders	Cross-breds	Indigenous
1.	Repeat breeding	68 (41.46)	21 (38.18)
2.	Anoestrous	34 (20.73)	10 (18.18)
3.	Metritis/endometritis	28 (17.07)	9 (16.36)
4.	Retained placenta	11 (6.70)	7 (12.72)
5.	Dystokia	8 (4.87)	6 (10.90)
6.	Prolapse of vagina/uterus	7 (4.26)	2 (3.63)
7.	Cystic ovaries	6 (3.65)	—
8.	Torsion of uterus	2 (1.22)	—
	Total	164 (100.00)	55 (100.00)

Note : Figures in parentheses are percentage to total.

bit of concentrate. It was well recognized that proper feeding of animals is essential to maintain their reproductive status. The incidence of uterine infections were about 17.07 and 16.36 per cent in cross-bred and indigenous cattle respectively. The infections gain entry into the reproductive system both in AI through unsterilized equipments and in natural service through infected bulls. In any case the cows, whether cross-bred or indigenous, are likely to be exposed to infection in the above ways, which might be the reason for the negligible difference in the incidence of metritis between cross-breds and indigenous animals.

The incidence of retained placenta was slightly higher in indigenous cows than in cross-breds as reported by the cattle owners. This indicated the poor feeding and high mineral deficiencies in local cows compared to cross-breds as these were the main reasons for the incidence of retention of placenta in cattle.

The results also revealed that dystokia was a problem encountered more often in indigenous cows than in cross-bred cattle. With the introduction of cross-breeding programme the indigenous cattle are being inseminated, especially with the semen of exotic bulls which are known for their heaviness. Such animals usually develop heavy foetuses which may lead to dystokia, whereas the cross-breds with proportionately larger pelvic capacity when inseminated with exotic or cross-bred semen do not face this problem of large sized foetuses which might be the reason for low incidence of dystokia in cross-bred cows.

The incidence of prolapse of vagina/uterus, cystic ovaries and torsion of uterus was very low in cross-bred cattle. But, in case of indigenous cattle the incidence of the above disorders appeared to be almost negligible. The above findings were in line with that of the revelations of Venkatasubramanian and Rao (1993).

Parasitic Disorders

Worm and tick infestation accounted for more than 87 per cent of the cases in cross-bred and indigenous cattle under parasitic disorders (Table 3.6). The differences in the incidence of worm and tick infestations in cross-bred and indigenous cattle was negligible. The incidence of worm and tick infestations mainly depend upon the level of management under which the animals are maintained. The high incidence of 12.06 per cent of schistosomiasis in indigenous animals was due to the farmers' practice of taking their work animals to community water tanks and grazing where the chances of getting this infestation were high, whereas low in cross-breds as they were mostly stall fed. The incidence of babesiosis and theileriosis, though low were reported only in cross-breds but not in indigenous cattle. The above finding was in conformity with the observations of Rao and Sohal (1985),

Venkatasubramanian and Rao (1993) and Venkatasubramanian (1994) who reported that incidence of theileriosis was noticed only in cross-breds and not in indigenous cattle or buffaloes.

Though there were reports of the incidence of anaplasmosis, especially in cross-breds in the veterinary institutes the farmers were not able to identify and report this disease. Hence the incidence of anaplasmosis was not observed in the present study. It was also possible that the number of cases of theileriosis as rcported by the farmers may include anaplasmosis cases, as it is not possible for them to differentiate between anaplasmosis and theileriosis.

Table 3.6. Incidence of Parasitic Disorders in Cross-breds and Indigenous Cattle

Sl. No	Type of Parasitic Disorders	Cross-breds	Indigenous
1.	Worm infestations	52 (53.06)	30 (51.72)
2.	Tick infestations	37 (37.81)	21 (36.20)
3.	Schistaosomiasis	5 (5.10)	7 (12.06)
4.	Babesiosis	2 (2.04)	—
5.	Theileriosis	2 (2.04)	—
	Total	98 (100.00)	58 (100.00)

Note : Figures in parentheses are percentage to total.

Respiratory Disorders

Bronchitis and pneumonia were the two important respiratory disorders mainly reported by the farmers among cross-breds and indigenous cattle (Table 3.7). The incidence of bronchitis was more a problem in cross-breds (65.51 per cent) than in indigenous cattle (54.16 per cent), whereas the percentage of pneumonia was high in indigenous animals than the cross-breds. The majority of the respiratory disorders were reported in calves and work bullocks. Poor housing and unhygienic practices associated with keeping of young calves along with the adult animals was the main reason for the higher incidence of respiratory disorders among calves, whereas in work bullocks the incidence was high because of exhaustion owing to rigorous work and inhalation of dust during work. Though there were differences in the incidence of bronchitis and pneumonia in cross-breds and indigenous cattle, the percentage of total animals reported to have suffered with these disorders was almost the same. This finding was in conformity with that of Venkatasubramanian and Rao (1993).

Table 3.7. Incidence of Respiratory Disorders in Cross-breds and Indigenous Cattle

Sl. No.	Type of Disorders	Cross-breds	Indigenous
1.	Bronchitis	19 (65.51)	13 (54.16)
2.	Pneumonia	10 (34.48)	11 (45.83)
	Total	29 (100.00)	24 (100.00)

Note : Figures in Parentheses are percentage to total.

Mammary Gland Disorders

Mastitis was reported in as high as 53 per cent of the cross-bred animals and 33 per cent of indigenous cattle under the category mammary disorders (Table 3.8). The higher incidence of udder oedema was seen among crossbreds (40.63 per cent) because of their high milk production capacity and poor milking management practices in the farm. The incidence of teat injuries in indigenous cattle was high due to frequent butting incidence during grazing. However, mammary gland disorders were not that significant as these accounted for about four per cent of the total ailments reported.

Table 3.8. Incidence of Mammary Gland Disorders in Cross-breds and Indigenous Cattle

Sl. No.	Mammary Disorders	Cross-breds	Indigenous
1.	Mastitis	17 (53.12)	6 (33.33)
2.	Udder oedema	13 (40.63)	4 (22.22)
3.	Teat injuries	2 (6.25)	8 (44.44)
	Total	32 (100.00)	18 (100.00)

Note : Figures in parentheses are percentage to total.

Mortality Percentage

The details of the mortality percentage among different categories of cross-bred and indigenous animals are provided in Table 3.9. It was evident from the table that total mortality rate was little lower than one per cent in both the groups of cattle. The mortality in calves of both cross-bred and indigenous cattle was about two per cent. The general poor care of cross-bred male calves and indigenous female calves resulted in the higher mortality rate in calves. However, the mortality rate was not that significant in both cross-breds and indigenous cattle. It was well within the normally expected rate when the total number of animals under the study was taken into consideration. This was mainly because of the timely vaccination of the animals by the animal husbandry and dairy development departments. Moreover, in general, the management conditions followed by the farmers presently were adequate enough to keep the mortality rate under check and the farmers practice of timely disposal of the sick or ailing animals and calves before their death.

Table 3.9. Mortality Rate (%) in Cross-breds and Indigenous Cattle

Sl.No.	Description of Cattle	Cross-breds	Indigenous
1.	Cows	0.3	0.2
2.	Bullocks	—	0.3
3.	Heifers	0.2	0.1
4.	Calves	2.4	2.6
	Total	0.86	0.66

Adding further woes to the above situation, the increased cost of milk production with respect to cross-bred cattle, urban-rural divide over the milk prices and large scale existence of unorganised milk marketing system led to the situation of lack of remunerative price to the producers which in turn seriously affects the growth of dairying in this country. Therefore, it is the need of this hour to eliminate all these threats and provide practical solutions to all these factors responsible for the negative development in this field.

The above analysis of Strengths, Weaknesses, Opportunities and Threats with respect to Indian dairy scenario given along with possible solutions to bring about desirable change will help the readers to arrive at a judicial understanding about the dairy development in the country by taking into consideration both positive and negative aspects associated with it.

Summary

Strengths refers to the basic assets or potentials of a thing that would provide competitive advantage for the growth and development. Weaknesses are the liabilities that can create a state of time and situation which acts on a specific disadvantage for its growth and development. Opportunities means the ability to grow and achieve the given specific objectives in a given direction and situation. Threats are the situations that block the ability to grow, develop and progress in a given situation. In this Chapter the SWOT analysis concept has been applied in the context of dairy development in the country. The analysis helps to understand our strengths with respect to dairying and consolidate the same. The weaknesses can be eliminated and the threats can be tackled smoothly. It also helps to understand the various opportunities to be utilised by us for the promotion of dairying in the country. As it gives the foresight and considerable evidence of pros and cons, the probability of lateral stage failures is bound to be considerably reduced.

References

Acharya, R.M. (1984). Constraints in Milk Production Enhancement in India, *Diamond Jubilee Souvenir* (1983-84), NDRI, Karnal.

Acharya, R.M. (1989). Cross-breeding Cattle as an instrument to increase milk production in rural areas, *Indian J. Anim. Sci.*, 59 (2): 264.

Cook, K.J. (1994). AMA Complete Guide to Strategic Planning for Small Business, NTC Publishers Group: Lincoln Wood, Illinois, U.S.A.

Gupta, K.K. and Dipak De (1989). A Comparative Study on Constraints Perceived by Adopters and Non-Adopters in Rearing Crossbred Cows in Jaipur District, Rajasthan, *Indian J. Dairy Sci.* 42(3): 456.

Kothai, K. (1993). SWOT Analysis of Rural Development Projects, *Indian Journal of Extension Education*, 29: 43-49.

Leonard, D.G.; Timothy, M.N. and William, J.P. (1993). *Applied Strategic Planning: A Comprehensive Guide*, McGraw Hill, Inc.

Mikkilinenin, V.K. (1976). *A Study of Adoption of Few Selected Dairy Practices in Upland and Delta Areas of Vijayawada Taluk*, Krishna District (A.P.), M.Sc. Thesis, Kurukshetra University, Karukshetra.

Nachiappan and Srinivasa Murthy (1976). The Impact of SFDA on the Knowledge of Participant Small Farmers of Tamil Nadu. *Indian J. Extn. Edu.* 13 (34) : 65-66.

Nayak, H.S.; Bajaj; S.S. and Raut, Dr. R. (1986). Problems of Dairy Farmers in Ahmednagar District of Maharashtra, *Maha. J. Extn. Edu.* 5: 107.

Patel, R.K.; Singh, C.B.; Sharma, P.A. and Manipal (1978). Constraints in Transfer and Adoption of New Technologies, Operational Research Project Report, NDRI, Karnal, p. 117.

Patel, B.T. (1980). *A Study of Factors Influencing Successful Functioning of Village Milk Producers Co-operative Societies in Kaira District of Gujarat*, Ph.D. Thesis, IARI, New Delhi.

Puthuswamy, T. (1976). *A Study of Knowledge, Adoption and Attitude of Small Farmers towards Mixed Farming in Sirsa and Arekal Taluka*. Ph.D. Thesis, HAU, Hissar.

Rao, B.S. (1975). *A Study of the Combined Impact of Dairy Co-operatives and ICDP on Socio-economic Changes in the Milkshed areas of Bhongir* (A.P.) M.Sc. Thesis, NDRI, Karnal.

Rao,. M.R. and Sastri, P.M. (1984). Prospects and Constraints in Milk Production Programmes through the Weaker Sections of the Rural Society, *Indian Dairyman*, 36(9) : 481.

Rao, S.V.N. and Sohal, T.S. (1985). Incidence and treatment of theileriosis in crossbreeds, *Dairy Guide*, 6 (8): 17-20.

Sharma, R.K. (1980). *A study of Socio-Psychological and Infrastructural Constraints in the Efficient Execution of ICDP*, Ph.D. Thesis, Kurukshetra University, Kurukshetra.

Sharma, K.N.S. and Jain, D.K. (1984). Factors affecting Prenatal Mortality in Bovines. I breed, year and season differences. *Indian J. Anim. Sci.*, 54 (4) : 297-300.

Singh, R.N.; Mishra, R.R. Dutta; O.P., Prabhakaran; V.T. and Malhotra, J.C. (1986). Health Disorders in Zebu and Exotic & Zebu crosses. *Indian J. Anim. Sci.*, 56 (12): 1229-33.

Sharma, R.K. and Makhija, V.K. (1991). Constraints encountered by Field Veterinarians in Implementing the Programme of ICDP. *Indian J. Dairy Science*, 49(7).

Sidhu, K.S. (1980). *A Study of the Dimensional Variation in the Knowledge of Dairy Farmers of ICDP and Non-ICDP Areas of Punjab*. M.Sc. Thesis, Kurukshetra University, Kurukshetra.

Subramanian, R. (1982). *A Study of Technological and Socio-economic Impact of Milk Co-operatives in Erode District of Tamil Nadu*. Ph.D. Thesis, Kurukshetra University, Kurukshetra.

Venkatasubramanian, V. and Ramchand (1991). Constraints : Dairy Development in India, *Milcow*, 13(3) : 3.

Venkatasubramanian, V. and Ramchand (1993). Socio-Psychological Constraints perceived by Field Veterinarians of Tamil Nadu, *Indian Veterinary Journal*, 70(5) : 472.

Venkatasubramanian, V. and Rao, S.V.N. (1993). Incidence of health disorders in cross-breds and indigenous cattle under field conditions. *Indian J. Dairy Sci.*, 46(7) : 302-306.

Venkatasubramanian, V. (1994). *Multidimensional Study on Cross-breeding Programme in Tamil Nadu*, Ph.D. Thesis, NDRI, Karnal.

Venkatasubramanian, V. and Fulzele, R.M. (1996). *Dairy Farming in Tropics*, MD Publications, 11, Darya Ganj, New Delhi-2.

Venkatasubramanian, V. and Bandyopadhyay, A.K. (1998). Agricultural Farming in Andaman and Nicobar Islands, *Technical Bulletin*, Central Agricultural Research Institute, P.B. 181, Port Blair-744101.

Venkateswarlu, K. and Kalla, J.C. (1996). *SWOT Analysis of NARP*, Delta Publishing House, 4, MCH Complex, Puttlibouli, Hyderabad-1.

PART II

MANAGEMENT IN DAIRY DEVELOPMENT PROGRAMMES

4

Managing Dairy Development Programmes in India

Management of human resources is felt very much important in any organisation and it is a fundamental aspect in the dairy development programmes. The dairy development is achieved through new knowledge and technologies produced by people which is implemented through people and adopted by people. Therefore, one of the most important tasks of achieving excellence in our dairy development programme is to develop a well trained personnel of the proper size, mix and educational level with adequate training to motivate them for an outstanding job performance. It is estimated that during the period 1980-1995 on an average only 2.87 per cent out of the total budget allotted was spent towards the human resources development activities by various research and development organisations involved in the dairy development. A common expectation among the dairy development workers is to update their performance through aquisition of new knowledge and skill. Therefore, a careful planning and implementation of human resources development in our dairy development programme is a key element for its success. Therefore, an analysis have been done with respect to various aspects of human resources management in the dairy development programmes to suggest suitable ways and means for its improvement for achieving an outstanding performance in our dairy development programmes.

Planning Human Resource Needs

Often the organisations involved in the dairy development plea for more and more staff ignoring the issues like proper mix of disciplines, levels of training and experience. As a result many of the R&D organisations are facing the problem of either over-staffing or under-staffing and unequal distribution of the experts. Therefore, careful planning for an optimum level of human resources is the fundamental challenge faced by our dairy development programmes.

Many of the organisations involved in the dairy development have too many people rather than too few, at least for the level of financial resources available. As a consequence, most of the budget is spent for personnel cost with the resultant shortage of operational funds. The shortage of funds for improvement in the quality of manpower employed, their travel and work facilities resulted in low levels of productivity.

The cause of unplanned staffing can be attributed to factors like lack of initial planning for staff requirements corresponding to the size of operation, inclusion or dropping up of programmes based on local/political pressures, employees negative attitude towards posting in remote areas, sanction of additional staff in certain departments due to the pressure from in and outside the organisation, lack of programme prioritisation and non-implementation of project based budgeting in our dairy development programmes. The above weaknesses have resulted in an uneven distribution of personnel and poor prioritisation in the use of limited resources. A myth seems to have developed in some organisations involved in dairy development that one can implement dairy development programme without professionals who are actually qualified in some aspects of dairying. The presence of unskilled professionals with inadequate knowledge in dairying is one of the serious constraints with respect to dairy development. For example, the promotion policy adopted by some organisations to promote group D or supporting staff employees into technical cadres by following roster system has resulted in the process of adding technicians without any required knowledge, skills and discipline to do dairy development work.

In addition, there are instances that the graduates without any fundamental degree in anyone of the disciplines concerned with dairying have been admitted into various post-graduate courses by just giving one year pre-requisite courses in respective disciplines. This has been practiced to overcome the shortage existed with respect to availability of manpower specialisation in various disciplines of dairying. When such practices have been started in times of acute shortage of dairy development professional it has come near to impossible at present to stop such courses. It is continuing even after the situation that surplus of adequately skilled manpower specialized in the disciplines of dairying holding M.Sc. and Ph.D. degrees are available. Therefore, a timely review of continuing the absorption of persons other than those who have got fundamental and specialized degrees in dairying is a must. The above practice of producing quacks in the name of meeting the shortage of manpower is to be curtailed immediately. All these above problems are direct result of lack of planning in human resources needs in the dairying sector. Therefore, the costs, both for the training and subsequent personnel costs have become too high for many institutions. Since such people are hired in substantial numbers salaries and benefits are, therefore, occupying a higher proportion in the available budget without any fruitful output resulting in the failure of the programmes.

The undue importance given to the managerial positions have resulted in the preference of such positions by the skilled professionals by acquiring additional management degrees or getting away elsewhere for such posts. This has resulted in poor skilled staff at the lower level. Therefore, when planning the human resource requirements, the importance associated with technical and skilled staff undertaking the work at lower and middle level shall not be neglected. This means ensuring that the proper importance with respect to the number, skill, mix and recognition of technical work is to be included in the staffing plan. Well qualified technical staff are essential component to maximize the outcome of the dairy development programmes. The problems of ill trained and non-professional technical staff, therefore, needs an immediate attention in the planning of human resource development in the dairy development programmes.

Evaluation of Job Performance

Evaluating the job performance of the personnel is an important factor associated with the job improvement programmes as it identifies and reinforces the strengths and minimise the effects of individual weaknesses.

Investigations revealed little relationship between the annual performance ratings generated by evaluators and actual on-the-job performance. When the same individual is evaluated by two or more evaluators, the assessments vary widely. It is certain that such evaluation will demoralise the employees and thereby his performance and job satisfaction will decrease. Therefore, the on-job evaluation provided to the employee has resulted in decreasing the performance rather than improving his work efficiency. It is much better to do the evaluation in a planned and scientific manner with a provision for the person being evaluated can understand his performance in every aspect of his job and identifies his own weaknesses and strengths. Since most of the time the annual evaluation is being done in a confidential manner, there is very little opportunity for the employees to improve their performance. In addition, an aim of suspicion, slavism, technical suppression by superiors, groupism, flattering of superiors and yes-bossism prevails in the organisation. Therefore, an open evaluation system with an employee participatory approach is needed to evaluate the actual job performance of the employee. In order to improve the job performance more reliably periodical evaluation based on actual job situation will be more useful than the annual confidential rating system which is being done as a ritual than to serve any positive purpose.

Bureaucracy and Technocracy

One of the thorny problem faced by all the technocrats in most of the dairy development organisations is the bureaucratic dominance over the technocracy. The common killing problem is the extension of civil administration system to the dairy development organisations instead of adopting development administration system. Most of the Indian technocrats have to think, act and report according to the wishes of his reporting officers or top boss. Therefore, in most of the organisations the technocrats feel that they and their work are not important and feel disgusted. It is also too painful to discuss that in India research managers drawn from technocrats also behaves in the same way as that of a bureaucrat from civil administration which has ultimately resulted in the research-technocrats-administrator functional gap.

It is best, therefore, for an ultimate survival of the dairy development programmes in the country a speedy recovery from the bureaucratic syndrome is necessary and the technocrats should be given the right recognition, freedom, responsibilities, status and participation in the management process than top down approach. An attitude that technocrats and the development programmes are there for the purpose of administrators need to be discouraged and the fact that the administrative mechanism is there to facilitate the programme needs to be realised at all levels.

Motivation for Excellence

The productivity usually means possession or use of the resources to create something. Today, productivity in science is linked with prosperity of a country. The dairy development is need based and goal oriented. Every government in the world is keen to increase their scientific achievements and set the goals to achieve technological independence. In Dairying sector, the technological independence achieved in our country is mainly due to the efforts of technocrats like Dr. V. Kurien and his team rather than any bureaucratic planning. Independence to technocrats lead to the technological independence. Presently, the world power is determined by the scientific knowledge and technological advancement possessed by a country. Irrespective of the size and availability of natural resources in the country, Japan could be able to emerge as a strong world power because of its technological advancements only. The scientific knowledge gets their recognition, importance, and economic value based on their ability to solve the problems. Solving the problems of dairy development in the country requires among other things, sufficiently motivated professionals involved in the programmes. Their good work is to be recognized in order to get quality output from them. What might a dairy development worker is to be provided with that could make him an effective professional? What might be the motivational constraints to be removed that could make him more effective and efficient? are some of the basic questions that confront all those responsible for dairy development in the country. To help and meet the need for an effective and intensive functioning of these skilled professionals, adequate performance motivation is, therefore, the first and foremost solution that can be thought of.

Nature of the Motivational Problems

While a number of attempts have been made to determine the job performance and job satisfaction of the industrial workers and managers, very little work has been done to determine the same with that of dairy development personnel. The job analysis is accomplished through first, a series of job observations and interviews to identify among other things, critical duties performed, the functional purposes of the duties and circumstances of conditions which facilitate or hinder the performance. Unless the professionals are well equipped to perform their duty, we cannot expect efficiency and satisfaction from their work and also it is very difficult for them to improve their level of performance as well as to upkeep their motivational level towards their jobs. In thinking about what is important in the job of a dairy development professional we must think about :

(i) The nature and level of motivation with which he is working.
(ii) How well a scientist can respond to the motivational constraints he encounters in attempting to do his job?

The job productivity and job satisfaction are important components in a job. The factors responsible for these components are :

(i) Personal factors,
(ii) Factors inherent in the job, and
(ii) Organizational or institutional factors.

According to Herzberg (1969), satisfiers and dissatisfiers are two separate and distinct factors associated with the jobs. The satisfiers include those positive factors such as achievement, recognition, responsibility, advancement and work itself, whereas the dissatisfiers include factors such as supervision, working conditions, interpersonal relationship, status, salary and job security. The absence of these factors bring dissatisfaction to the employee, so the name dissatisfiers.

Some of the motivational constraints faced by the dairy development personnel are lack of rewards and inadequate recognition of good work, poor promotional policies, inadequate career growth opportunities due to lack of clear cut policies, inadequate opportunity for training and skill development, lack of participation in programme planning, inadequate freedom to work, rigid administrative rules and red-tapism, inadequate infrastructural facilities at grassroot level and economic inadequacy.

Positive Motivation

The positive motivation is largely accomplished by creating right value system within the organizational culture and constantly reinforcing these values. A work environment in which all are aware that their services are going to make an important difference in the lives of millions of poor people is a tremendous stimulus. The second task is to take various actions that will make each individual that he or she is making an important contribution to the noble goal of improving the life of poorest of the poor. Employees should not be under the illusion that only very few in their organisation are important and contributing something useful but that each one of them is an important worker in the mission against hunger and poverty. When employees have the sense that what they are doing is much more than their jobs and that they are the worthy contributors to their organisations' goal, they will be motivated to give their maximum effort.

The essence of dairy development is the art and science of dealing with people. Without good and well-motivated staff, the best facilities and most-adequate financial resources remain unproductive. With people who have been carefully selected to do specific tasks, who have been well informed as to what is expected out of them, who are skilfully coached to do that task; and above all, who are highly motivated, there is almost no limit to what can be accomplished, even with less than ideal facilities and budgets.

Motivation involves making people know they are doing something important; treating them as individuals who can be trusted to perform responsibly; recognizing their achievements; and surrounding them with an environment conducive to performance and productivity.

Issues related to Job Satisfaction

Job satisfaction is derived from and is caused by many inter-related factors associated with the job. The success of various dairy development programmes depends upon the extent of interest and satisfaction the dairy development workers derive from their jobs. Keeping this in view a study was conducted to determine the level of job satisfaction among the dairy development professionals and also to assess the contribution of various job factors in influencing the job satisfaction level.

The average job satisfaction score of the professionals indicated that majority of the professionals (69 per cent) have medium level of job satisfaction. It was only 17 per cent of the professionals reported a high level of job satisfaction. This leads to conclude that majority of the professionals neither satisfied nor dissatisfied with their jobs. Infrastructural, recognition, growth and economic constraints are the four major factors responsible in determining the job satisfaction of the dairy development professionals.

The results emphasised the need for adequate economic benefits in the form of allowances and incentives along with dynamic infrastructural facilities and suitable rewards in recognition of the excellent work performed. In addition, adequate promotional avenues need to be created to raise the job satisfaction level of dairy development professionals in the country.

Summary

Improving the management process of our dairy development programmes need three levels of attention, i.e. an overall general strategies and specific techniques. The focus is to be made on humam resources. Human resources need to be given much importance than financial or physical resources. The planning and development of human resources is to be given paramount importance. The concern for human resources is to be manifested in three interrelated strategies. First, employees are to be offered participation in the management process. Second, the organisation's philosophy concerning employee's needs and the values of co-operation and team work are to be well articulated. Third, close attention is to be given to fit the right person at the right place in the organisation.

The specific techniques to be adopted are right and transparent performance appraisal system, emphasis on work groups and team work, open communication and less red-tapism, consciences in decision making, relief from bureaucratic approach and concern for the employee at all levels of the organisation.

Change is difficult but it is a must. Bringing about a constructive change in the management policies of dairy development programmes will certainly bring about a faster growth rate in this sector which is the need of the hour.

References

Benis, W. and Narus B. (1985). *Leaders: The Strategies of Taking Charge.* Harper and Row, New York.

Bergnes, G.J. and Honey, W.V. (1966). *Organisational Relations and Management Action*, McGraw Hill, New York.

Drucker, P.F. (1966). *The Effective Executive*, Harper and Row, New York.

Elz, D. (1984). The Planning and Management of Agricultural Research, The World Bank, Washington DC.

Grensing, L. (1985). *How to Evaluate Employees in a Realistic Way*, Comm. Briefings, Blachwood, New Jersey.

Myers, I. and Briggs, K. (1962). *Introduction to Type, Consulting Psychologies and Press.* Palo Alto, California.

Nickel, J.L. (1983). *Workshop on Agricultural Research Policy and Management*, 26-30. Sept., Port of Spain, Trinidad.

Nickel, J.L. (1989). Managing People, in : *Research Management for Development*, IICA, Sanjose, Costa Rica.

Ranftl, R.M. (1985). *Training Managers of High Productivity*, Hughes Aircraft Co., Los Angeles, California.

Rao, S.V.N. (1984). *Correlates of Job Performance of Veterinary Surgeons Working in ICDP Karnal.* Ph.D. Thesis. N.D.R.I., Kurukshetra University, Kurukshetra.

Venkatasubramanian, V. (1991). *Professional Constraints Perceived by Field Veterinarians of Tamil Nadu*, M.Sc. Thesis, NDRI, Karnal.

5

PERFORMANCE OF MILK CO-OPERATIVES
An Analysis of Success and Failure

In India, dairying, like all agricultural enterprises, rests with the individuals as small size units. Most of the farmers belong to the small or marginal category, owning two or three cattle and less than two hectares of land. These farmers are scattered all over the country and are vulnerable to a variety of forces peculiar to the dairy industry (Mescarenhas, 1988). India accounts for about one-sixth of the cattle and half of the buffalo population of the world. In spite of this large population, the per cattle milk production is one of the lowest in the world. There is a ten-fold difference in declared milk output per cow from approximately 500 kg per annum in India to over 5,000 kg in North America and some European countries (*Dairy India*, 1992).

The pace of dairy development in India picked up only after 1970 with the launching of Operation Flood. This period saw the emergence of dairy co-operatives as the dominant force. The Dairy Industry, after years of neglect became producer oriented. Milk Producers were assured of reasonable markets for increased milk production. India's milk production has now more or less tripled. Presently, India has emerged as the number one producer of milk in the world. Conversion of seasonal surpluses into milk powder and its recombination into milk in the lean months became a part of the national strategy for dairy development. This ensures adequate returns to the farmers for their seasonal surplus and year round availability of milk at reasonable price to the consumers (Aneja, 1994).

The marketing of milk produced by these dairy farmers depends on three major outlets, *i.e.*, milk vendors, private milk plants, and milk co-operatives. The first two outlets have been perceived to be exploitative by the dairy farmers (Singh, 1992). The third outlet for milk is least exploitative and organised by the producers. Its real significance was understood only when the integrated system of dairy co-operatives was evolved at Anand (Gujarat) and then extended to other parts of the country.

The Anand Model of co-operative structure is built on a vertically integrated single industry co-operative that links rural producers with urban consumers by introducing intensive milk production model, improved technology and marketing. The "Anand Model" has come to mean a three-tier organisational structure linking primary producers societies responsible for procurement to district co-operative unions engaged in processing and product manufacturing while at State level district unions are grouped together into federations charged with the co-ordination of functions. In 1986, an All India Federation (NCDF), was added to this structure for the purpose of policy co-ordination at the national level.

The first phase of the Operation Flood Programme (OF-I) was operated between 1970 and 1980. The funds needed for its implementation were generated by the sale of donated stock of butter oil and skimmed milk powder after recombination into milk for the benefit of India's urban population. These aid commodities, in turn, were freely obtained from EEC's surplus stocks and donated through the World Food Programme. OF-I covered 8 rural districts, later extended to 27 districts, and involved the participation of 1.4 million rural families. The main objective of OF-I was to capture a commanding share of the metropolitan milk markets, namely, Delhi, Calcutta, Bombay and Madras. The second phase of Operation Flood, launched in 1979, aimed at bringing much wider areas of India within its range. OF-II was to link 147 major towns to rural milk-sheds, thereby covering 155 districts and 10 million milk producers.

OF-II was financially supported by both the EEC (Dairy aid commodities) and the World Bank (Financial aid). In 1986, Operation Flood-III was proposed by the Indian Government to the EEC and the World Bank to further extend and consolidate the infrastructure for milk procurement, processing and marketing established under OF-I and OF-II. Operation Flood-III is to be implemented up to 1994. Growth of Village Milk Producers Co-operative Societies (VMPCSs) under Operation Flood Programme is already given in Chapter-1.

Another step was taken in 1989 to augment rural income through the launching of Technology Mission on Dairy Development. It aims to apply modern technology to improve productivity facilities for cattle improvement in terms of breeding farms, bull mother farms, semen freezing and artificial insemination facilities, veterinary hospitals, etc., available with the State Animal Husbandry Departments and OF. In addition, the ICAR Institutes and State Agricultural Universities have also participated to provide the research back-up.

The decision to transfer the Anand type dairy co-operatives to other parts of India was a recognition of the importance of lessons learnt at Anand. The people involved and the situations cannot be recreated as each setting will be unique, but what remains is the concept of the dairy co-operatives and how it can be transplanted to other regions. In transferring the concept under OF-I and OF-II, a core group of people who have been trained at Anand have formed a nucleus for transferring the Anand type VMPCS to the whole country.

The National Commission on Agriculture (1976) indicated that most of the co-operatives have failed to develop properly. Doubts have been expressed about the efficacy of co-operative structure for development of dairying in the country. This has happened despite the fact that in most of the developed countries of the world, dairying is based on co-operative organisation. Sidhu and Sidhu (1990) revealed that 'Anand Pattern' which was highly successful in Gujarat

State, when introduced in Punjab had not proved to be very successful due to different socio-economic conditions in the two States.

Statement of the Problem

There are reports that milk co-operatives have done remarkably well in Gujarat (6.5% of total milk production in 1989-90) as compared to other States (Bhanja, 1981; Subramanian, 1982; Gopal, 1983; Dabas, 1984; Singh, 1987). Milk co-operatives could not prove their mettle in other States of the country especially in major milk producing States like Uttar Pradesh (17.8% of total milk production in 1989-90), Punjab (9.7% of total milk production in 1989-90) and Haryana (6.1% of total milk production in 1989-90) (XXIV DIC, p. 18). Their poor performance could be attributed to various factors such as: irregular payments, malpractices by secretaries, lack of technical persons, competition by vendors, political interference and unconducive socio-personal, psychological, organisational and environmental factors. Similarly, the good performance of milk co-operatives in State like Gujarat might be due to some other factors which needs to be validated. Thus, there was a need to ascertain various factors responsible for the performance of milk co-operatives.

In the light of above observations, following research questions can be framed:

(a) Why milk co-operatives were performing better in Gujarat and not in Haryana?
(b) How to measure the performance of milk co-operatives?
(c) What were the characteristics of the farmer members affecting the performance of milk co-operatives?
(d) How organisational and environmental factors influenced the performance of milk co-operatives?
(e) What were the reasons for the failure of milk co-operatives?
(f) What were the constraints in the functioning of milk co-operatives?

Significance of the Study

Development planners in many countries are continuously searching ways of generating equitable and self-sustaining projects. India's Operation Flood experience has often appealed to their imagination as a potential model for income generating and poverty combating activities. The present study aimed to find out the individual, socio-economic, environmental and organisational differences between the milk co-operatives of Gujarat and Haryana. The Gujarat State was selected being pioneer in the field of milk co-operatives and Haryana being a State with high milk production, but where milk co-operatives are not working well, it helped to find out indicators of performance of milk co-operatives. An index to measure the performance of milk co-operatives was developed. The factors responsible for the performance of milk co-operatives were identified. This study will help the research scholars, scientists, milk co-operative officials and other government and semi-government organisations engaged in dairy development to know the performance of milk co-operatives and to undertake measures for improving the performance of milk co-operatives. In order to answer the questions related to the performance of milk co-operatives, the present study entitled, *Performance of Milk Cooperatives in Haryana and Gujarat — A Comparative Study* was planned with the following objectives:

(1) To develop an index for measuring the performance of milk co-operatives.

(2) To compare the variability in the socio-personal, economic and psychological characteristics of members of milk co-operatives.

(3) To study the effect of organisational and environmental factors on the success and failure of milk co-operatives.

(4) To identify constraints in the functioning of milk co-operatives.

Limitations of the Study

The present study is confined to 14 selected village milk producers co-operative societies (in two States of Gujarat and Haryana) due to time and resource constraints. The findings of the study are based on the expressed responses of the respondents which might not be completely free from their individual biases and prejudices. However, every care has been taken to obtain objective, reliable and valid responses by applying the relevant methodological techniques. Despite the above limitations, sincere attempts and considerable thoughts have been exercised in making the study as objective as possible.

Locale of the Study

Gujarat and Haryana States were purposively selected for the present study. Gujarat State was selected being the pioneer in milk co-operative sector and the Haryana State was selected being a representative State with high milk production potential, but where milk co-operatives are not working well.

Sampling Procedure

From the milk co-operative federations of both the selected States one milk union with best performance (as rated by the federation) was selected. Thus, two milk unions selected for this study were: Ambala from Haryana and Mehsana from Gujarat.

Selection of the Block/Taluka

From each selected Dairy Co-operative Milk Producer's Union one revenue unit, viz. Barara Block from Ambala and Visnagar Taluka from Gujarat, were selected randomly for the study.

Selection of the Village Milk Producers' Co-operative Societies (VMPCSs)

Two types of VMPCSs were selected for this study. Firstly, the functional VMPCSs; and secondly, the defunct VMPCSs.

Selection of the Functional Village Milk Producers' Co-operative Societies

All VMPCSs of Barara Block and Visnagar taluka registered between 1985 to 1988 (in order to select VMPCSs of similar age) and remained functional till the data collection (January 1993 to June 1993) were ranked on the basis of performance index developed for the study). On the basis of performance score, all the VMPCSs were classified into two groups, i.e., one group of VMPCSs above the medium performance score and other group below it. Then from each group three VMPCSs were selected randomly. Thus, a total of 12 functional VMPCSs (six from each State) were selected for the study (Details in Table 5.1).

Selection of Defunct VMPCSs

Two defunct VMPCSs were to be selected from each Block/ Taluka but records showed no defunct VMPCS in Visnagar. So, data from two defunct VMPCs of Barara Block only were obtained for the purpose of this study (Given in Table 5.1).

Selection of the Respondents

Respondents were selected from DCMPU, functional VMPCSs and defunct VMPCSs as per the procedure given below:

Respondents at Union Level

From each selected DCMPU, ten employees were selected randomly with the criteria that Head (General Manager/Chief Executive Officer) of the Union was selected and at least one employee from every major section of the union was

Table 5.1. Selection of VMPCSs

Sr. No.	Level	Selection criteria	Locale 1	Locale 2	Total
1.	State (Federation)	Purposive	Haryana	Gujarat	2
2.	District (DCMPU)	Best Performance	Ambala	Mehsana	2
3.	Block/ Taluka	Random Selection	Barara	Visnagar	2
4.	Village (VMPCS)				
	(a) Functional	Performance Index	1. Galleri 2. New Binjalpur 3. Khanpura 4. Adpodh Musalmanan 5. Adarsh Dera Salimpur	1. Bokarwada 2. Thumthal 3. Sunshi 4. Rathodipura 5. Bajipura	12
	(b) Defunct	Two Latest Defunct	1. Kamabas 2. New Sarakpur	Not Reported	2

included in the sample, thus a total of 20 DCMPU employees (10 each from Ambala DCMPU and Mehsana DCMPU) were selected for this study.

Respondents from Functional VMPCS

Two types of respondents selected from functional VMPCS was prepared and the farmer members were categorised into low, medium and high milk suppliers based on the quantity of milk supplied by them to the VMPCS using cumulative square root technique. A total of 180 farmer-members (90 from each State) were selected using probability proportional to size technique, subject to the condition that a minimum of 20 members were to be selected from each category.

Selection of Management Committee Members

From each selected functional VMPCS five management committee members were selected randomly. Thus, a total of 60 (30 from each State) management committee members were selected for this study.

Respondents from Defunct VMPCSs

From every selected defunct VMPCS, 12 ex-farmer members were selected randomly. In Gujarat, no defunct VMPCS was found.

Variables and their Measurement

Keeping in view the objectives of the study, the relevant variables for the present study were selected on the basis of review of literature, consultations with experts and experience gained in the pilot study. The variables studied and their measurements are listed in Table 5.2. The variables with their operational definitions and measurement procedure are given below:

Organisational Factors

1. Milk collection business, 2. Performance traits

Environmental and Infrastructural Factors

1. Village Infrastructure, 2. Population Characteristics, 3. Location Characteristics

Member-Farmers Traits

1. Socio-personal, 2. Economic, 3. Psychological, 4. Communicational, 5. Perception of constraints

Managing Committee Members Traits

1. Socio-personal, 2. Economic, 3. Psychological, 4. Communicational

DCMPU Employees

1. Perception of constraints
2. Perceived by member farmers
3. Perceived by DCMPU employees

Indicators of Performance of VMPCS

1. Increase/decrease in membership
2. Average price in rupees per litre of milk paid to the member-farmers
3. Average quantity of milk collection per member
4. Percentage of households covered by VMPCS in the whole village

Table 5.2. List of Variables and their Measurement Selected for the Investigation.

Sr. No.		Variable	Measurement
A.	**Dependent Variable**		
		Performance of VMPCS	Index developed
B.	**Independent Variables**		
(i)	***Village Environment***		
	(a)	*Village Infrastructure and Agricultural Resources:*	
	(i)	Village Infrastructure	Bhanja (1981)
	(ii)	Total Agricultural Land of Village	Village Records
	(iii)	Land of Village under Irrigation	- do -
	(b)	*Population Characteristics:*	
	(i)	Village Population	- do -
	(ii)	Village Infrastructure	- do -
	(iii)	Land under Irrigation	- do -
	(c)	*Location:*	
	(i)	Distance from Chilling Centre on Milk Route	- do -
	(ii)	Type of Road Link	- do -
	(iii)	Distance from Milk Plant	- do -
	(d)	*Milk Collection:*	
	(i)	Milk Collecting Agencies	Direct Question
	(ii)	Daily Milk Collection of Different Agencies	Schedule Prepared

Table 5.2 (*Contd.*)

Sr. No.	Variable	Measurement
	(iii) Price offered by Milk Collecting Agencies	- do -
	(iv) Average Daily Milk Collection Business per Household	- do -
(ii)	***Organisational Variables concerning VMPCS***	
	(i) Number of Farmer-Members for Last Three Years	VMPCS Records
	(ii) Number of Members Supplying Milk for Last Three Years	- do -
	(iii) Total Number of Paid Employees for Last Three Years	- do -
	(iv) Total Volume of Business in Rupees for Last Three Years	- do -
	(v) Quantity of Milk spoiled during Last Three Years	- do -
	(vi) Manpower per One Lakh Rupees Business for Last Three Years	Bhanja (1981)
	(vii) Supplies and Services Provided by VMPCS during Last Three Years	VMPCS Records
(iii)	***Primary Member Variables***	
	(a) Socio-Economic Variables:	
	(i) Age	Direct Question
	(ii) Herd Size	- do -
	(iii) Milk Production	Schedule Prepared
	(v) Milk Sale	- do -
	(vi) Value of Assets	- do -
	(b) Psychological Variables:	
	(i) Economic Motivation	Modified Scale of Supe (1969)
	(ii) Attitude Towards VMPCS	Verma (1993)
	(c) Communicational Variables:	
	(i) Mass Media Exposure	Schedule Prepared
	(ii) Extension Contact	- do -
(iv)	***Variables concerning Management Committee Members of VMPCS***	
	(a) Socio-Economic Variables:	
	(i) Age	Direct Question
	(ii) Value of Assets	Schedule Prepared
	(b) Psychological Variables:	
	(i) Commitment towards VMPCS	Modified Scale of Porter *et al.* (1974)

Table 5.2 (*Contd.*)

Sr. No.		Variable	Measurement
	(ii)	Political Knowledge and Affiliation	Bhanja (1981)
	(c)	*Communicational Variables:*	
	(i)	Mass Media Exposure	Schedule Prepared
	(ii)	Extension Contact	- do -
(v)		***Variables concerning Farmer-Members of Defunct VMPCS***	
	(a)	*Socio-Economic Variables:*	
	(i)	Age	Direct Question
	(ii)	Value of Assets	Schedule Prepared
	(b)	*Psychological Variables:*	
	(i)	Economic Motivation	Modified Scale of Supe (1969)
	(ii)	Attitude Towards VMPCS	Verma (1993)
	(iii)	Perceived Reasons for Failure of VMPCS	Direct Question
(vi)		***Constraints:***	
	(i)	Constraints in the Functioning of VMPCS and DCMPU as perceived by Member-Farmers of VMPCS	Direct Questions
	(ii)	Constraints in the Functioning of DCMPU and VMPCS as perceived by DCMPU Employees	- do -

Dependent Variable

Performance of VMPCS

According to Khandalwalla (1977), "Organisational performance is a net result of the combined efforts of all individuals and groups in the organisation". Organisational performance is as ambiguous a term as organisational goal. Since it is difficult to define exactly what the goals of an organisations are, so it is also difficult to determine how well the organisation has performed. In assessing organisational performance, we are forced to ask the following question: Performance from whose view-point? Take, for example, a firm. From society's view-point efficient production of products or services needed by society may be said to be the goal of the firm and so the firm should be evaluated in terms of whether it does this or not. From the point of view of the owners of the firm, profitability and growth rate may be the criteria for assessing performance. From the point of view of the employees of the firm, the firm's performance may be assessed in terms of how well it treats its employees. From the point of view of the firm's customers, courteous service, prompt delivery, a good product and a competitive price may be the criteria in terms of which the firm's performance is assessed (Khandalwalla, 1977).

However, for present study, the variable 'Performance of VMPCS' was operationalised as the performance of the VMPCS with respect to selected indicators of performance, viz., increase or decrease in membership, average price in rupees per litre of milk paid to the members, average quantity of milk collection per member, and percentage of households covered by VMPCS in the whole village. These indicators were selected to measure performance of VMPCS after literature consultation, discussion and investigation. Accordingly, a performance index was developed as given below:

Computation of Performance Score

The detailed method of preparation of performance index is given under following sub-heads:

1. Selection of indicators of performance,
2. Assigning weightage to selected indicators,
3. Key to scoring of indicators,
4. Calculating score of indicator, and
5. Computing the performance score of VMPCS.

1. Selection of Indicators of Performance

After thorough literature consultation, discussion with scientists, research scholars, VMPCS employees and investigators, following four indicators were selected to assess the perfcrmance of a VMPCS:

(1) Yearly increase or decrease in membership over a period of three years.
(2) Yearly quantity of milk collection in litres per member per year over a period of three years.
(3) Average quantity of milk collection in litres per member per year over a period of three years.
(4) Percentage of households covered by a VMPCS in a year in the whole village over a period of three years.

2. Assigning Weightage to Selected Indicators

The selected indicators were subjected to judgement of 25 employees of "The Kurukshetra and Karnal Co-operative Milk Producers' Union Ltd., Karnal". These employees were given a schedule and requested to rank the indicators with 1, 2, 3, 4 rank considering 1 to be the least important and 4 to be the most important indicator of performance of a VMPCS. After rating of indicators by judges, the total score of each indicator was calculated by summing up the rank given to each indicator by 25 judges. Now, the indicator with the maximum score was given the weightage 4 and accordingly in the decreasing order of scores the remaining indicators were given a score of 3, 2 and 1 (Details given in Table 5.3). Thus, the selected indicators were given the weightage as given below :

	Indicators	Weightage (W)
(a)	Yearly average of milk price in rupees per litre paid to the members over a period of three years	4
(b)	Average quantity of milk collection in litres per member per year over a period of three years	3
(c)	Percentage of households covered by a VMPCS in a year in the whole village over a period of three years	2
(d)	Yearly increase or decrease in membership over a period of three years.	1

3. *Key to Scoring of Indicators*

Key scores to each indicators were assigned on the basis of discussion with scientists and research scholars as follows:

	Indicators	Key Scores (KS)
(a)	Yearly increase or decrease in membership over a period of three years.	1, 2, 3, 4, 5
(b)	Yearly average of milk price in rupees per litre paid to the members over a period of three years	1, 2, 3, 4
(c)	Average quantity of milk collection in litres per member per year over a period of three years	1, 2, 3, 4
(d)	Percentage of households covered by a VMPCS in a year in the whole village: over a period of three years.	1, 2, 3, 4

Note : Details given in Table 5.4.

4. *Calculating the Indicator Score*

The score of individual indicator was calculated by the formula:

$$IS = \Sigma\ KS \times W$$

where,

IS is the indicator score,

KS is the key score, and

$\Sigma KS = \Sigma Ks_i;\ \Sigma Ks_i = Ks_1 + Ks_2 + Ks_3$

where,

Ks_1 is the key score for first year,

Ks_2 is the key score for second year,

Ks_3 is the key score for third year, and

W is the weightage assigned to the indicator.

(Example given in table 5.3)

Table 5.3. Method of Assigning Weightage to Selected Indicators of Performance of VMPCS

DMPU Employee Member	Ranks of Indicators			
	A	B	C	D
1	2	4	3	1
2	1	4	2	3
3	1	3	2	4
4	4	2	3	1
5	2	4	3	1
6	3	1	4	2
7	2	4	3	1
8	2	4	1	3
9	1	3	4	2
10	2	4	3	1
11	2	4	1	3
12	1	3	4	2
13	2	4	1	3
14	1	4	2	3
15.	1	2	2	5
16	1	4	3	2
17	1	3	2	4
18	1	3	4	2
19	1	3	4	2
20	2	4	3	1
21	1	2	3	4
22	4	3	2	1
23	1	4	2	3
24	2	3	4	1
25	1	3	2	4
Total	42	82	67	59
Weightage	1	4	3	2

where,

A= Yearly increase or decrease in membership over a period of three years.

B= Yearly average of milk price in rupees per litre paid to the members over a period of three years.

C= Average quantity of milk collection in litres per member over a period of three years.

D= Percentage of households covered by a VMPCS in a year in the whole village over a period of three years.

Table 5.4. Key to Scoring of Indicators of Performance of VMPCS

Sr. No.	Indicators	Score
A.	Yearly increase or decrease in membership over a period of three years:	
	(a) More than 50 per cent decrease	1
	(b) Up to 50 per cent decrease	2
	(c) Static	3
	(d) Up to 50 per cent increase	4
	(e) More than 50 per cent increase	5
B.	Yearly average of milk price in rupees per litre paid to the members over a period of three years:	
	(a) Up to Rs 3.00	1
	(b) Rs 3.01 to Rs 3.50	2
	(c) Rs 3.51 to Rs 4.25	3
	(d) Above Rs. 4.25	4
C.	Average quantity of milk collection in litres per member per year over a period of three years:	
	(a) Up to 500	1
	(b) 501 - 1000	2
	(c) 1001 - 2000	3
	(d) Above 2000	4
D.	Percentage of households covered by a VMPCS in a year in the whole village over a period of three years:	
	(a) Up to 30	1
	(b) 31 to 45	2
	(c) 46 to 70	3
	(d) Above 70	4

5. Computing the Performance Score of a VMPCS

The performance score (PS) of each VMPCS was calculated by the formula:

$$PS = \Sigma IS_i$$

where,

PS is the performance score of a VMPCS, and

$$\Sigma IS_i = Is_1 + Is_2 + Is_3 + Is_4$$

where,

Is_1 is the indicator score for first indicator of VMPCS,
Is_2 is the indicator score for second indicator of VMPCS,
Is_3 is the indicator score for third indicator of VMPCS,
Is_4 is the indicator score for fourth indicator of VMPCS,
(Example given in Table 5.5).

Table 5.5. Computing the Performance Score of VMPCS

Name of:

VMPCS	....	A	....
Secretary	....	B	....
Block/Taluka	....	C	....
District	....	D	....
State	....	E	....

1. Yearly increase or decrease in membership over a period of three years:

Year	*Increase/decrease over previous year*	*Score*
1988-89	Static	3
1989-90	10% increase	4
1990-91	9% increase	4

$IS_1 = 11 \times 1 = 11$

2. Yearly average of milk price in rupees per litre paid to the members over a period of three years:

Year	*Average Price*	*Score*
1988-89	5.20	4
1989-90	5.62	4
1990-91	5.89	4

$IS_2 = 12 \times 4 = 48$

3. Average quantity of milk collection in litres per member per year over a period of three years:

Year	*Average Milk Collection*	*Score*
1988-89	915	2
1989-90	1094	3
1990-91	1130	3

$IS_3 = 8 \times 3 = 24$

Contd.

Table 5.5 (*Contd.*)

4. Percentage of households covered by a VMPCS in a year in the whole village over a period of three years:

Year	Per cent Household Covered	Score
1988-89	45	2
1989-90	60	3
1990-91	90	4

$IS_4 = 9 \times 2 = 18$

$$PS = IS_1 + IS_2 + IS_3 + IS_4 = 11 + 48 + 24 + 18 = 101$$

$$\text{Performance} = PS/MPS \times 100 = 101/123 \times 100 = 82.11\ \%$$

where,

PS is performance score, and

MPS is maximum possible (performance) score.

Independent Variables

Village Infrastructure

It refers to different public institutions and facilities available in the village, viz., Panchayat, School, Youth Club, Credit Society, Mahila Mandal, Post Office, Police Station, Electricity, Medical Aid Centre, Stockman Centre, Veterinary Dispensary, Village Market and Availability of Water. One score was given to each facility available and zero score was given to each facility not available in the village. It was measured by the schedule prepared by Bhanja (1981). Maximum obtainable score was 16 and minimum was zero. The scores given against each facility were added to represent the village infrastructure score.

Total Agricultural Land of Village

It refers to the sum total of the cultivable land in possession of all the villagers in hectares in one village. This was recorded from village records.

Land of Village Under Irrigation

It is the sum total of irrigated cultivable land in possession of all the villagers in hectares in one village. This was recorded from village records.

Population Characteristics

Village Population

It is the sum of all the men, women and children in the villages. It was recorded from the village records.

Total Number of Households

It refers to the sum total of number of individual households in the village. It was recorded from the village records.

Family Type

It refers to the number of joint families and nuclear families in the village. Here, nuclear family denotes a family with husband, wife and children only. Whereas, the joint family is a family with husband, wife, their mothers, fathers, brothers, sisters, and married or unmarried children. It was recorded from the village records.

Dominant Caste

It refers to a particular caste in the village which dominates in most of the village activities and whose opinion influences the decision of villagers on community matters. It was asked directly from the villagers. From the number of dominant caste people, percentage was calculated.

Number of Literate Persons

It refers to the sum total of men, women and children above six years of age who can read and write. Literacy percentage of village was calculated from the number of literate persons of the village. This was reported from the village records.

Location Characteristics

Distance from Chilling Centre on Milk Route

It refers to the distance of village from nearest chilling centre on milk route in kilometres. This was recorded from VMPCS records.

Type of Road Link

Refers to the type of road, i.e., Kaccha, Pucca or mixed, starting from milk collection centre of village to the main road leading to the milk plant. It was recorded from VMPCS records.

Distance from Milk Plant

It refers to the location of nearest milk plant (Co-operative/ Private) from milk collection centre of village in kilometres. It was recorded from VMPCS records.

Milk Collection

Milk Collection Agencies

It refers to the number of milk collecting agencies operating in the village at the time of data collection. It was asked directly from VMPCS employees. Three agencies were found collecting milk from the village, viz., VMPCS, vendors and milk contractors.

Daily Milk Collection of Different Agencies

It refers to average quantity of milk collected in litres by different milk collecting agencies per day in the year previous to inquiry in a village. It was measured with the help of formula:

DMC = Highest milk collection in litres last year + Lowest milk collection in litres last year/2

The data regarding highest and lowest milk collection were recorded from the village sources.

Price Offered by Milk Collecting Agencies

It refers to the price offered per litre of milk by different milk collecting agencies on the previous day of inquiry. It was noted from the village sources.

Average Daily Milk Collection Business Per Household

It refers to the average daily milk collection business (in rupees) of cow or buffalo milk by different milk collecting agencies in the village. It was calculated by the formula:

$$ADMC = DMC \times P / NH$$

where, *ADMC* is average daily milk collection business (in rupees) of cow or buffalo milk of an agency. *DMC* is, average daily milk collection of that agency. *P*, is the price in rupees per litre of milk offered for cow or buffalo milk by that agency and *NH* is the total number of households in the village concerned.

Organisational Variables Concerning VMPCS

Number of Farmer-Members for the Last Three Years

It refers to the number of farmer-members registered with VMPCS for last three years from the year of inquiry, i.e. 1988-89, 1989-90 and 1990-91. It was noted from VMPCS records.

Number of Farmer-Members Supplying Milk for the Last Three Years

It refers to number of registered farmer-members who were actually supplying milk to the VMPCS for the last three years from inquiry, i.e. 1988-89, 1989-90, 1990-91. It was noted from VMPCS records.

Quantity of Milk Spoiled during the Last Three Years

It refers to the average quantity of milk in litres spoiled in a year for the last three years from inquiry, i.e. 1988-89, 1989-90, 1990-91. It was recorded from VMPCS records.

Total Number of Paid Employees for the Last Three Years

It refers to the number of paid employees employed by the VMPCS in a year. The data were recorded for three years i.e., 1988-89, 1989-90 and 1990-91 from VMPCS records.

Total Volume of Business in Rupees for the Last Three Years

It refers to the volume of business of VMPCS including its sale and purchase activities in rupees in a particular year. The data were recorded for three years, i.e. 1988-89, 1989-90 and 1990-91 from VMPCS records.

Manpower Per One Lakh Rupees Business for the Last Three Years

It was related to the number of persons available with the VMPCS to undertake its business in a year. The data were recorded for three years, i.e. 1988-89, 1889-90 and 1990-91 from VMPCS records. It was calculated by the formula given by Bhanja (1981):

Manpower = Total number of paid employees / Total volume of business in rupees × 1,00,000

Supplies and Services provided by VMPCS during Last Three Years

It refers to the amount of supplies and services such as A.I., emergency visits, quantity of fodder seed sold, tours, cattle shows, and film shows, etc. organised/provided by the VMPCS to its member-farmers in a year. The data were collected for three years, i.e. 1988-89, 1989-90 and 1990-91 from VMPCS records.

Socio-Economic Variables

Age

It refers to the chronological age of the respondent on the basis of English calendar. It was measured by direct questioning. The respondents were categorized as:

(a) Young = Less than (Mean – S.D.)
(b) Middle aged = Between (Mean – S.D.) to (Mean + S.D.)
(c) Old aged = Above (Mean + S.D.)

Herd Size

It refers to the total number of dairy animals (milch/draft) of any age possessed by the respondent at the time of inquiry. Each animal was given one score. On the basis of scores obtained the herd size of respondents was categorised as:

(a) Small = Less than (Mean – S.D.)
(b) Medium = Between (Mean – S.D.) to (Mean + S.D.)
(c) Large = Above (Mean + S.D.)

Milk Production

It refers to the quantity of milk produced in litres by one household on a day prior to inquiry. It was measured with the help of a schedule. The respondents on the basis of milk production were categorised as:

(a) Low = Less than (Mean – S.D.)
(b) Medium = Between (Mean – S.D.) to (Mean + S.D.)
(c) High = Above (Mean + S.D.)

Milk Consumption

It refers to the quantity of milk consumed in litres by one household on a day prior to investigation. It was measured with the help of a structured schedule. The respondents on the basis of milk consumption were categorised as:

(a) Low = Less than (Mean – S.D.)
(b) Medium = Between (Mean – S.D.) to (Mean + S.D.)
(c) High = Above (Mean + S.D.)

Milk Sale

It refers to the quantity of milk produced in litres by the household on a day prior to inquiry. It was measured with the help of a schedule on the basis of milk sale in litres. The respondents were categorised as:

(a) Low = Less than (Mean – S.D.)
(b) Medium = Between (Mean – S.D.) to (Mean + S.D.)
(c) High = Above (Mean + S.D.)

Value of Assets

It was operationalised as approximate value of assets (value of land, houses, ornaments, bank accounts and per year earnings from service/business/agriculture, etc.) in rupees possessed by the respondent (his wife and children, if living together) at the time of inquiry. It was measured with the help of a structured schedule. The respondents on the basis of the value of their assets were categorised as:

(a) Low = Less than (Mean – S.D.)
(b) Medium = Between (Mean – S.D.) to (Mean + S.D.)
(c) High = Above (Mean + S.D.)

Psychological Variables

Economic Motivation

It relates to the occupational success in terms of profit maximisation and the relative value an individual places on the economic end. However, for present study it referred to economic compulsion of the farmer to join and continue with the VMPCS. It was measured by the modified scale of Supe (1969) containing six statements. Some of the statements were positive and some were negative. The method of scoring was as follows:

Statements	Response				
	Strongly agree	Agree	Undecided	Disagree	Strongly disagree
Positive	7	5	4	3	1
Negative	1	3	4	5	7

The respondents on the basis of their economic motivation score were categorised as:

(a) Low = Less than (Mean – S.D.)
(b) Medium = Between (Mean – S.D.) to (Mean + S.D.)
(c) High = Above (Mean + S.D.)

Attitude towards Village Milk Producers' Co-operative Society

According to Kretch and Crutchfield (1948), attitude is defined as the tendency to respond either favourably, unfavourably or indifferently to certain persons, objects, situations or ideas. Whereas, for the present study, attitude towards VMPCS has been operationalised as the tendency of the individual member-farmer of a VMPCS to respond either favourably, neutrally or unfavourably towards VMPCS. The scale of Verma (1993) was used to measure this variable which contained 12 statements. Some of the statements were positive and some were negative. The scoring for these statements was done as given below:

Statements	Response		
	Agree	Undecided	Disagree
Positive	3	2	1
Negative	1	1	3

On the basis of the scores obtained by the respondents they were categorised as:

(a) Unfavourable = Less than (Mean – S.D.)
(b) Neutral = Between (Mean – S.D.) to (Mean + S.D.)
(c) Favourable = Above (Mean + S.D.)

Commitment towards VMPCS

Commitment refers to the feeling of responsibility or obligation towards any object, person, ideology or organisation. Whereas, for the present study, it refers to an innate or induced feeling of responsibility, dedication and obligation of management committee members towards the village milk producers' co-operative society. It was measured by the modified scale of Porter *et al.* (1974) containing fifteen statements. Some statements were positive and some were negative. The scoring method for this variable was as follows:

Statements	Response				
	Strongly agree	Agree	Undecided	Disagree	Strongly disagree
Positive	5	4	3	2	1
Negative	1	2	3	4	5

The respondents on the basis of scores obtained for commitment towards VMPCS were categorised as:

(a) Low = Less than (Mean – S.D.)
(b) Medium = Between (Mean – S.D.) to (Mean + S.D.)
(c) High = Above (Mean + S.D.)

Political Knowledge and Affiliation

Political affiliation refers to the level of association with political parties of the respondent and political knowledge refers to knowledge of respondent regarding political events and personalities at local and national levels. It was measured by the schedule prepared by Bhanja (1981) containing seven questions. The respondents were categorised on the basis of scores obtained for political knowledge and affiliation as given below:

(a) Low = Less than (Mean – S.D.)
(b) Medium = Between (Mean – S.D.) to (Mean + S.D.)
(c) High = Above (Mean + S.D.)

Communicational Variables

Mass Media Exposure

It refers to thebhb bn participation/utilisation of mass media like newspapers, printed material, radio, exhibition and television etc. It was measured with the help of a schedule containing four statements regarding the frequency of use of different mass media. The scores given to different frequencies were as under :

Frequency	Daily	Once a week	Once a fortnight	Once a month	Rarely	Never
Score	5	4	3	2	1	0

It also contained two statements regarding number of films and *melas*/exhibitions seen in the previous year to inquiry. The scores given for different responses were as:

Response	One	Two	More than two
Score	1	2	3

The respondents on the basis of scores obtained for mass media exposure were classified as:

(a) Low = Less than (Mean – S.D.)
(b) Medium = Between (Mean – S.D.) to (Mean + S.D.)
(c) High = Above (Mean + S.D.)

Extension Contact

It refers to both acquaintance and frequency of contacts with extension personnel. It was measured with the help of a schedule containing seven statements regarding the frequency of contacts with different extension personnel and the scoring was done as given below:

Frequency	Regularly	Occasionally	Rarely	Never
Score	3	2	1	0

The respondents on the basis of scores obtained for extension contact were categorised as under:

(a) Low = Less than (Mean – S.D.)
(b) Medium = Between (Mean – S.D.) to (Mean + S.D.)
(c) High = Above (Mean + S.D.)

Constraints and other Variables

Constraints in the functioning of VMPCS and DCMPU as perceived by Member-Farmers of VMPCS

The simplest dictionary meanings of constraints are: to force, to confine, to restrict the motion, to restrain, to oppress, to limit, coersion, repression of natural behaviour; the act or action of using force or threat of force to prevent or condition an action, or state of being checked, restricted to avoid or perform some action.

Constraints exist primarily in terms of how they are defined and conceived in an organisation (Bhople and Agrawal, 1987; Twade *et al.*, 1987). Constraints are projections of collective sentiments rather than simple mirrors of objective conditions (Bora, 1990). According to some authors, there exists interaction among the different constraints (Hashim, 1989). It is argued that many constraints exist simultaneously in several stages of development and patterns of progress from one stage to another depending upon the time, place and other sets of conditions (Bhatnagar, 1974 and Mishra *et al.*, 1987).

Bhople and Agrawal (1987) defined constraint as the state or quality of sense being restricted to a given course of action or constraints are nothing but the problems that come in the way of adoption of technology.

However, for the present study, constraints refer to all the factors hindering the smooth and efficient functioning of VMPCS. It was asked directly from member-farmers by an open question. These constraints were categorised into the following categories after tabulation and listed on the basis of frequency as following:

Constraints	Frequency Category of milk supplier			
	Low	Medium	High	Total
1. Social				
2. Economical				
3. Organisational				
4. Psychological				
5. Technological				

Constraints in the functioning of DCMPU and VMPCS as perceived by DCMPU Employees

It refers to all those factors hindering the smooth functioning and efficient coordination of DCMPU and VMPCS as perceived by the employees of DCMPU. It was asked directly from DCMPU employees and the perceived constraints were categorised on the basis of frequencies as:

Constraints	Frequency
1. Social	
2. Economical	
3. Organisational	
4. Psychological	
5. Technological	

Perceived Reasons for Failure of VMPCS by Members of Defunct VMPCS

It refers to the factors responsible for the failure of a functional VMPCS as perceived by the ex-members of a defunct VMPCS. It was asked directly from these members and categorised on the basis of frequency as:

Perceived Reason	Frequency
1. Social	
2. Economical	
3. Organisational	
4. Psychological	

Data Collection

Preparation and Pre-testing of Interview Schedule

A structured interview schedule was prepared including all the variables on which information was required to fulfil the objectives of the study. The schedule was prepared by consulting literature, scientists, research scholars and DCMPU and VMPCS employees. This schedule was pre-tested in the non-sample area and accordingly necessary changes were made in the final schedule.

Final Data Collection

The research data were collected by personal interview from selected respondents and reliable secondary sources during January 1993 to August 1993. The respondents were contacted at DCMPU, VMPCS, at their homes and at their farms. Necessary precautions were taken to establish rapport and to obtain reliable and relevant information. The co-operation of the president of VMPCSs, supervisors of VMPCSs, DCMPU employees, VMPCS employees, and formal and informal leaders of the area was availed to locate, establish rapport, and communicate with the farmers. Their presence during the actual interview was avoided as far as possible except while interviewing respondents of Gujarat not knowing Hindi or English.

Statistical Analysis

The data were analysed by applying suitable statistical techniques in a systematic manner to get the results. The data collected for different categories of respondents were tabulated and subsequently, transferred to master sheet. The data analysis was done at the Computer Centre of National Dairy Research Institute, Karnal. Following statistical tools were applied to analyse the research data.

Simple Statistics

Simple statistics like frequency distribution, percentage, mean standard deviation, cumulative square root, rank analysis etc. were used for the analysis of data.

Test of Significance for Comparison of Mean Score

In order to assess the variability in the socio-personal, economic and psychological characteristics of farmer-members and management committee members of Haryana and Gujarat States and to test the significance in the difference of mean scores of two States, '*t*' test was used.

Design of the Study

Research design refers to the plan structure and strategy employed to obtain the answers to the research questions. The design explains us what to observe, how to observe and how to analyse the observations. In the present study, an *ex post facto* research design has been used. The literal meaning of *ex post facto* is "from what is done afterwards". Kerlinger (1964) defined *ex post facto* research as "systematic empirical inquiry in which the scientist does not have direct control of independent variables, because their manifestations have already occurred or because they are inherently not manipulable. Inferences about relations among variables are made, without direct intervention, from concomitant variation of independent variables."

Findings of the Study

The data were collected and analysed according to the objectives of the study. The study focused on the comparative performance of milk co-operatives in Haryana and Gujarat. It dealt with the preparation and comparison of performance index, socio-personal, economic, psychological and communicational traits of member-farmers, management committee members of functional VMPCSs, and member-farmers of defunct

VMPCSs of Haryana and Gujarat States. It also aimed to find out variability in the infrastructural facilities, location characters, population characters and milk collection business traits. Finally, the constraints in the functioning of VMPCSs and factors responsible for the failure of VMPCSs have been identified. The results of the study are accordingly organised and presented under the following topics :

- Comparative profile of member-farmers and management committee members of Haryana and Gujarat.
- Comparative performance indices for VMPCSs in Haryana and Gujarat.
- Comparative variability of different traits affecting performance of VMPCSs in Haryana and Gujarat.
- Effect of different factors on the success of milk co-operatives in Haryana and Gujarat.
- Factors responsible for failure of VMPCSs.
- Comparative constraints in functioning of VMPCSs and DCMPUs.

Comparative profile of member-farmers and management committee members of Haryana and Gujarat.

The profile of the respondents (member-farmers of functional VMPCSs, management committee members of functional VMPCSs, and member-farmers of defunct VMPCSs) highlights their salient traits and these traits are assumed to affect the performance of VMPCSs. The variables under investigation were analysed critically and their primary description have been presented under the following sub-heads:

- Comparative profile of selected member-farmers of functional VMPCSs of Haryana and Gujarat.
- Comparative profile of selected management committee members of functional VMPCSs of Haryana and Gujarat.

— Profile of selected member-farmers of defunct VMPCSs of Haryana.

Comparative profile of selected member-farmers of functional VMPCSs of Haryana and Gujarat

Age

Age of an individual relates to one's ability to work, his critical analysis of situation and sound decision making. A perusal of Table 5.6 revealed that majority of the respondents (70% in Haryana and 72.22 per cent in Gujarat) belonged to middle age group followed by young (15.66% in Haryana and 13.33% in Gujarat) and old age (11.33% in Haryana and 14.14% in Gujarat). Thus, more young age member-farmers of VMPCSs were reported from Haryana. These findings were in line with those of Singh (1984), Verma (1993) and Singh (1994).

Herd Size

It can be observed from Table 5.6 that average herd size was same in both the States. Majority of members (74.74%) were having medium herd size followed by large (14.14%) and small (11.12%) herd size in both the States, which showed that dairy animals were an essential component of assets of majority of the farmers in both the States and the farmers were medium herd holders.

The above findings supported the earlier findings that majority of the respondents possessed medium herd size, viz., Verma (1988), Singh (1989), Verma (1993), Singh (1994) and Venkatasubramanian and Fulzele (1996).

Milk Production

A glance at Table 5.6 indicated that majority of the members were producing 3.5 to 14.0 litres of milk (medium) daily followed by high (16.66% in Haryana and 13.13% in Gujarat) milk production and low (7.77% in Haryana and 13.13% in Gujarat) milk production. This indicated that average member-farmers of Haryana produced more milk daily than average member-farmers of Gujarat.

Milk Consumption

It is clearly enunciated in Table 5.6 that majority of member-farmers households consumed medium (0.25 to 5.50 litres per day) quantity of milk followed by high (more than 5.50 litres per day) quantity in both thc States. No farmer-member household was found consuming low (less than 0.25 litre of milk per day) in Haryana as well as in Gujarat. Milk consumption per household was higher in Haryana in comparison to Gujarat.

Milk Sale

It is evident from Table 5.6 that majority (78.88% in Haryana and 73.33% in Gujarat) of the member-farmers sold medium quantity of milk per day. The result showed that on an average Gujarat member-farmers sold larger proportions of milk produced than member farmers of Haryana.

Value of Assets

It is apparent from Table 5.6 that most of the member farmers were having medium (between Rs. 3,90,740 and 9,88,565) value assets at the time of inquiry. The result also indicated that the average value of assets of member-farmers of Haryana was more than the value of assets of Gujarat member-farmers.

Economic Motivation

As depicted in Table 5.6 majority (58.88% in Haryana and 55.55% in Gujarat) of member-farmers were having medium level of economic motivation, followed by high (22.22% in Haryana and 33.33% in Gujarat) level of economic motivation, and low (18.88% in Haryana and 11.12% in Gujarat) level of economic motivation (less than 30 score).

This showed that member-farmers with high economic motivation to join VMPCSs were more in Gujarat in comparison to Haryana, which might be due to the fact that profitability from agricultural lands is more in Haryana compared to Gujarat.

Attitude towards Village Milk Producers' Co-operative Society

It may be visualised from Table 5.6 that majority (45.55% in Haryana and 44.44% in Gujarat) of the member-farmers were having neutral attitude towards VMPCS, followed by favourable (28.88% in Haryana and 33.33% in Gujarat), and unfavourable (25.57% in Haryana and 22.22% in Gujarat) attitude. Gujarat member-farmers possessed more favourable attitude towards VMPCS than Haryana member-farmers, which might be due to their different organizational, economic and socio-personal traits.

Mass Media Exposure

The results in Table 5.6 indicated that majority (67.77% in Haryana and 62.22% in Gujarat) of member-farmers had medium exposure to mass media. The farmer-members exposed to high mass media were 18.8 per cent in Haryana and 22.22 per cent in Gujarat. These results indicated that farmer-members exposed to high mass media were more in Gujarat than in Haryana which might be due to their different levels of attitude, interests, needs and opportunities to interact with different mass media. Similar results were reported by Singh (1984), Verma (1983) and Singh (1994) wherein they stated that majority of the dairy farmers had medium level of mass media exposure. The findings contradicted with Sheoran (1987) who stated that majority of the respondents had low exposure to mass media.

Table 5.6. Profile of the member farmers

S.No.	Traits	Categories	Range	Haryana		Gujarat	
				Frequency	Percentage	Frequency	Percentage
1	2	3	4	5	6	5	6
I.	**Socio-Economic**						
1.	Age (years)	Young	Below 30	15	16.66	12	13.33
		Middle	30 - 56	63	70.00	65	72.22
		Old	Above 56	12	13.33	13	14.44
2.	Herd Size (No.)	Small	Below 2	10	11.12	10	11.12
		Medium	2 - 8	67	74.44	67	74.44
		Large	Above 8	13	14.14	13	14.14
3.	Milk Production (litres)	Low	Below 3.5	7	7.77	12	13.13
		Medium	3.5 - 14.0	68	75.55	66	73.33
		High	Above 14.0	15	16.66	12	13.13
4.	Milk Consumption (litres)	Low	Below 0.25	0	0.00	0	0.00
		Medium	0.25 - 5.50	69	76.66	79	87.77
		High	Above 5.50	21	23.33	11	12.22
5.	Milk Sale (litres)	Low	Below 1.75	7	7.77	8	8.88
		Medium	1.75 - 9.75	71	78.88	66	73.33
		High	Above 9.75	12	13.33	16	17.77
6.	Value of Assets (Rs.)	Low	Below 390740	34	37.77	18	20.00
		Medium	390740 - 988565	30	33.33	65	72.22
		High	Above 988565	26	28.88	7	7.77

Contd.

Table 5.6 (*Contd.*)

1	2	3	4	5	6	5	6
II.	**Psychological**						
1.	Economic Motivation (score)	Low	Below 30	17	18.88	10	11.12
		Medium	30 - 40	53	58.88	50	55.55
		High	Above 40	20	22.22	30	33.33
2.	Attitude towards VMPCS (score)	Unfavourable	Below 27	23	25.57	20	22.22
		Neutral	27 - 35	41	45.55	40	44.44
		Favourable	Above 35	26	28.88	30	33.33
III.	**Communicational**						
1.	Mass Media Exposure (score)	Low	Below 5	12	13.33	14	15.55
		Medium	5 - 14	61	67.77	56	62.22
		High	Above 14	17	18.88	20	22.22
2.	Extension Contact (score)	Low	Below 7	27	30.00	8	8.88
		Medium	7 - 13	53	58.88	73	81.11
		High	Above 13	10	11.12	9	10.00

Extension Contact

It may be visualized from Table 5.5 that majority of the farmers fell in medium category of extension contact, followed by low and high extension contacts in both the States.

Member-farmers with high extension contact were slightly more in Haryana than in Gujarat which might be due to the fact that extension contact was more important for agricultural practices (other than animal husbandry and dairying) for Haryana farmers than Gujarat farmers.

The above findings were in line with the findings of Verma (1988). These findings did not agree with those of Singh (1984) who stated that majority of the respondents had high level of extension contact.

Comparative Profile of Selected Management Committee Members of Functional VMPCSs of Haryana and Gujarat

Age

A perusal of Table 5.7 revealed that majority of members (53.33% in Haryana and 56.66% in Gujarat) were of middle aged followed by old aged in Haryana (33.33%) and in Gujarat (26.66%). The members in young age category were 13.33 per cent in Haryana and 16.66 per cent in Gujarat. Thus, management committee members of old age were more in Haryana and of young age were more in Gujarat.

Value of Assets

Value of assets represents a person's socio-economic status in the society which reflects his socio-personal and psychological characteristics. As depicted in Table 5.7, majority of members were having medium value (between Rs. 3,90,740 and 9,88,565) of assets followed by low value (below Rs. 3,90,740) of assets in Haryana and Gujarat. The members with high value of assets (above Rs. 9,88,565) were 26.66 per cent in Haryana and 10.00 per cent in Gujarat. This showed that members with high value of assets as well as low value of assets were more in Haryana in comparison to Gujarat. It might be due to the productive and larger sizes of agricultural lands with Haryana farmers.

Commitment towards VMPCS

Commitment is a measure of dedication of management committee members towards VMPCS. It may be observed from Table 5.7 that most of the members (56.66% in Haryana and 50.00% in Gujarat) were having medium level of commitment towards VMPCS followed by high level of commitment level in Haryana (16.66%) and in Gujarat (30.00%). The low level commitment was found in 26.66 per cent members in Haryana and 20.00 per cent members in Gujarat. Thus, higher level of commitment among management committee members was found in Gujarat which might be due to the differences in socio-personal, economic and psychological traits of management committee members of the two States.

Political Knowledge and Affiliation

These traits reflect a person's awareness, aspiration and general outlook. It is apparent from Table 5.7 that majority (73.33% in Haryana and 53.33% in Gujarat) of the management committee members were having medium level of political knowledge and affiliation followed by low political knowledge and affiliation in Haryana (16.66%) and in Gujarat (30.00%). The high level political knowledge and affiliation was recorded in 10.00 per cent management committee members of Haryana and in 16.66 per cent management committee members of Gujarat.

These results revealed that management committee members with high level of political knowledge and affiliation were more in Gujarat which supports the deep rooted and matured leadership in milk co-operatives of Gujarat.

Table 5.7. Profile of the Management Committee Members

S.No.	Traits	Categories	Range	Haryana		Gujarat	
				Frequency	Percentage	Frequency	Percentage
I.	**Socio-Economic**						
1.	Age (years)	Young	Below 30	4	13.33	5	16.66
		Middle	30 - 56	16	53.33	17	56.66
		Old	Above 56	10	33.33	8	26.66
2.	Value of Assets (Rs.)	Low	Below 3,90,740	15	50.00	11	36.66
		Medium	3,90,740 - 9,88,565	7	23.33	16	53.33
		High	Above 9,88,565	8	26.66	3	10.00
II.	**Psychological**						
1.	Commitment towards VMPCS (score)	Low	Below 61	8	26.66	6	20.00
		Medium	61 - 72	17	56.66	15	50.00
		High	Above 72	5	16.66	9	30.00
2.	Political Knowledge & Affiliation (score)	Low	Below 8	5	16.66	9	30.00
		Medium	8 - 15	22	73.33	16	53.33
		High	Above 15	3	10.00	5	16.66
III.	**Communicational**						
1.	Mass Media Exposure (score)	Low	Below 5	8	26.66	6	20.00
		Medium	5 - 14	17	56.66	18	60.00
		High	Above 14	5	16.66	6	20.00
2.	Extension Contact (score)	Low	Below 7	6	20.00	2	6.66
		Medium	7 - 13	22	73.33	21	70.00
		High	Above 13	2	6.66	7	23.33

Mass Media Exposure

A glance at Table 5.7 indicated that more than 55.00 per cent members (in both the States) were having medium exposure to different mass media, followed by low exposure (26.66% in Haryana and 20.00% in Gujarat), and high exposure to mass media (16.66% in Haryana and 20.00% in Gujarat). Members with high mass media exposure were more in Gujarat which might be due to differences in interests, motivations, opportunities and priorities of management committee members of the two States.

Extension Contact

The results in Table 5.7 revealed that most of the management committee members were having medium level extension contact, followed by high level extension contact (6.66% in Haryana and 23.33 per cent in Gujarat) and low level extension contact in Haryana (20.00%) and in Gujarat (6.66%). These results indicated that management committee members having high extension contact were approximately four times more in Gujarat than in Haryana which showed the eagerness of Gujarat farmers towards the new innovations.

Profile of Selected Member Farmers of Defunct VMPCSs of Haryana

As there was no defunct VMPCS in randomly selected Taluka of Gujarat (Visanagar, Mehsana District), member-farmers of defunct VMPCS were selected and studied only in Haryana (Barara Block, Ambala District) and their profile is given below:

Age

It may be observed from Table 5.8 that majority (54.16%) of members were of middle age, followed by old age (25.00%) and young age (20.83%).

Value of Assets

A perusal of Table 5.8 revealed that most of the member-farmers were having medium value assets (between Rs. 3,90,740 and 9,88,565), followed by members with low value (below Rs. 3,90,740) assets and high value (above Rs. 9,88,565) assets. Thus around one-third members were having high value of assets which might be the cause for their low economic motivation towards VMPCSs.

Economic Motivation

It is apparent from Table 5.8 that 70.83 per cent members were having medium level of economic motivation, followed by low economic motivation (25.00%) and high economic motivation (4.16%). These results indicated that very few members were having high economic motivation for VMPCSs, which seems to be a prominent reason for the failure of VMPCSs in Haryana.

Attitude towards VMPCSs

It may be visualised from Table 5.8 that majority (70.83%) of the members were having neutral attitude towards VMPCSs followed by favourable attitude (16.66%) and unfavourable attitude (12.05%). Thus, attitude of the members of defunct VMPCSs was similar to the member-farmers of other functional VMPCSs.

Mass Media Exposure

It is evident from Table 5.8 that maximum member farmers (79.16%) were exposed to medium level of mass media, followed by low mass media exposure (12.50%) and high mass media exposure (8.33%). These results showed that mass media exposure of members of defunct VMPCSs was lower than that of the member-farmers of functional VMPCSs.

Table 5.8. Profile of Farmer-Members of Defunct VMPCSs (Haryana, N=24)

S. No.	Traits	Categories	Range	Haryana	
				Frequency	%age
I.	**Socio-Economic**				
1.	Age (years)	Young	Below 30	5	20.83
		Middle	30 - 56	13	54.16
		Old	Above 56	6	25.00
2.	Value of Assets (Rs.)	Low	Below 3,90,740	8	33.33
		Medium	3,90,740 - 9,88,565	9	37.50
		High	Above 9,88,565	7	29.16
II.	**Psychological**				
1.	Economic Motivation (score)	Low	Below 30	6	25.00
		Medium	30 - 40	17	70.83
		High	Above 40	1	4.16
2.	Attitude towards VMPCS (score)	Unfavourable	Below 27	3	12.50
		Neutral	27 - 35	17	70.83
		Favourable	Above 35	4	16.66
III.	**Communicational**				
1.	Mass Media Exposure (score)	Low	Below 5	3	12.50
		Medium	5 - 14	19	79.16
		High	Above 14	2	8.33
2.	Extension Contact (score)	Low	Below 7	3	12.50
		Medium	7 - 13	18	75.00
		High	Above 13	3	12.50

Extension Contact

The results in Table 5.8 indicated that most of the member-farmers (75.00%) were having medium level of extension contacts followed by low level extension contacts (12.50%), and high level extension contacts (12.50%). These results followed similar patterns as in other functional VMPCSs. Thus, low extension contact alone does not seem to be responsible for failure of VMPCSs in Haryana.

Comparative Performance Indices of VMPCSs in Haryana and Gujarat

Based on the indicators of performance of selected VMPCSs, a performance index was prepared for Haryana and another for Gujarat (details given in Methodology). Twelve VMPCSs were selected from Gujarat and six from Haryana. The descriptions have been presented under the following sub-heads:

(1) Performance Index for VMPCSs of Haryana.
(2) Performance Index for VMPCSs of Gujarat.
(3) Comparison of Performance Index between Haryana and Gujarat.

Performance Index for VMPCSs of Haryana

It may be visualised from Table 5.9 that performance pattern of different VMPCSs selected from Haryana presented in ascending order was—Galleri (44.71%), New Tandwali (52.03%), Tandwal Adarsh (56.09%), New Binjalpur (57.72%), New Dheen (58.53%), New Rukdi (60.16%), Chail Majra (60.97%), New Shimla (61.78%), Khanpura (63.41%), Rao Majra (66.66%), Adhoya Musalmanan (67.47%) and Adarsh Dera Salimpur (78.98%) (Fig. 5.1).

Table 5.9. Performance Index of VMPCSs of Haryana (N=12)

S. No.	Name of VMPCS	Performance score	Performance Percentage
1.	Galleri (S)	55	44.71
2.	New Tandwali (S)	64	52.03
3.	Tandwal Adarsh	69	56.09
4.	New Binjalpur (S)	71	57.72
5.	New Dheen	72	58.53
6.	New Rukdi	74	60.16
7.	Chail Majra	75	60.97
8.	New Shimla	76	61.78
9.	Khanpura (S)	78	63.41
10.	Rao Majra	82	66.66
11.	Adhoya Musalamanan (S)	83	67.47
12.	Adarsh Dera Salimpur (S)	91	73.98
	Mean	74.16	60.29

Where, *N* is the number of VMPCS of the selected Block/Taluka registered between 1985 to 1998.
(*S*) is the VMPCS selected for further study after sampling.
Maximum possible performance score for a VMPCS is 123.

Thus, performance ranged from 44.71 to 73.98 per cent with an overall mean performance percentage of 60.29 per cent in selected VMPCSs of Haryana (Fig. 5.1).

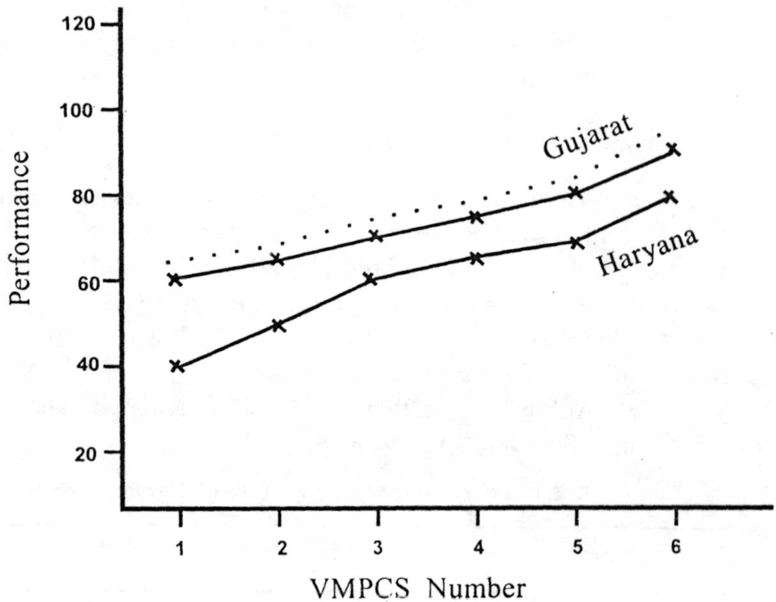

Fig.5.1. Performance of Selected VMPCSs of Haryana and Gujarat

Performance Index for VMPCSs of Gujarat

The performance pattern of different VMPCSs selected from Gujarat is presented in the following ascending order: Bokarwada (60.97%), Thumthal (68.29%), Vadu (68.29%), Sunshi (75.60%), Rathodipura (80.48%) and Bajipura (82.11%). The range of performance varied from 60.97 to 82.11 per cent with an overall mean performance percentage of 72.62 per cent. Thus Gujarat VMPCSs outperformed Haryana VMPCSs (Tables 5.10 and 5.9).

Table 5.10. Performance Index of VMPCSs of Gujarat (*N*=6)

S. No.	Name of VMPCS	Performance score	Performance percentage
1.	Bokarwada (*S*)	75	60.97
2.	Thumthal (*S*)	84	68.29
3.	Vadu (*S*)	84	68.29
4.	Sunshi (*S*)	93	75.60
5.	Rathodipura (*S*)	99	80.48
6.	Bajipura (*S*)	101	82.11
	Mean	89.33	72.62

Where, *N* is the number of VMPCS of the selected Block/Taluka registered between 1985 to 1998.
(*S*) is the VMPCS selected for further study after sampling.
Maximum possible performance score for a VMPCS is 123.

Comparison of Performance Index between Haryana and Gujarat

It may be observed from Table 5.11 that mean performance percentage of selected VMPCSs was 60.29 per cent in Haryana and 72.62 per cent in Gujarat, and the overall average was 66.45 per cent. Thus, performance of VMPCSs was significantly higher (12.33% higher) in Gujarat in comparison to Haryana. Further, mean performance gap in selected VMPCSs was 39.71 per cent in Haryana and 27.38 per cent in Gujarat and the overall mean performance gap was 33.54 per cent (Table 5.10).

The better performance of Gujarat VMPCSs might be due to the cumulative effect of a number of factors like socio-personal, economic and psychological characteristics of member-farmers, management committee members, and the organisational and other associated factors of VMPCSs and DCMPUs.

Table 5.11. Comparative Performance of Selected VMPCSs of Haryana (N=12) and Gujarat (N=6)

S. No.	State	Mean Performance Score	Mean Performance Percentage	Mean Performance Gap (%)
1.	Haryana	74.16	60.29	39.71
2.	Gujarat	89.33	72.62	27.38
	Average	81.74	66.45	33.54

Comparative variability of Different Traits Affecting Performance of VMPCSs in Haryana and Gujarat

It was expected that some of the characteristics of the respondents of two selected States (Gujarat and Haryana) would differ and vary significantly. In order to see whether the difference in the mean scores of different variables concerning farmer-members, management committee members, village infrastructure and VMPCSs variables were significant or not, '*t*' test was applied. Detailed description of variability has been presented under following sub-heads:

(1) Variability in the socio-personal, economic and psychological characteristics between member-farmers of Haryana (N=90) and Gujarat (N=90).

(2) Variability in the socio-personal, economic and psychological characteristics between management committee members of Haryana (N=30) and Gujarat (N=30).

(3) Variability in the village infrastructure and VMPCSs variables between Haryana (N=6) and Gujarat (N=6).

Variability in the Socio-Personal, Economic and Psychological Characteristics between Member-Farmers of Haryana (N=90) and Gujarat (N=90)

It may be seen from Table 5.12 that mean scores of some variables were differing significantly, some were differing significantly high and some were differing non-significantly.

The variables differing non-significantly as reflected by

Table 5.12. Variability in the Socio-Personal, Economic and Psychological Characteristics between Member-Farmers of Haryana (N=90) and Gujarat (N=90)

S. No.	Trait	Mean Value		't' value
		Haryana	Gujarat	
1.	Age (Years)	40	43	1.452
2.	Herd Size (No.)	5.5	5.0	1.031
3.	Daily Milk Production per Household (Litres)	8.76	8.36	0.497
4.	Daily Milk Consumption per Household (Litres)	3.81	1.95	5.018**
5.	Daily Milk Sale per Household (Litres)	4.94	6.41	2.459*
6.	Total Value of Assets at the Time of inquiry (Rs.)	8,93,224	4,27,974	4.220**
7.	Economic Motivation (Score)	33	39	9.037**
8.	Attitude towards VMPCS (Score)	30	31	0.960
9.	Mass Media Exposure (Score)	10.25	8.00	3.280**
10.	Extension Contact (Score)	8.25	11.00	7.640**

* Significant at 0.05 level of probability.
** Significant at 0.01 level of probability.

mean scores and confirmed by '*t*' values were aged (40 and 43 years), herd size (5.5 and 5.0), daily milk production per household (8.76 and 8.36 litres) and attitude towards VMPCS (30 and 31 score) for Haryana and Gujarat States respectively.

The variable differing significantly (at 0.05 level of probability) was daily milk sale per household, with a mean score value of 4.94 litres for Haryana and 6.41 litres for Gujarat.

The variables with highly significant (at 0.01 level of probability) mean score difference were: daily milk consumption per household (3.81 and 1.95 litres), total value of assets at the time of inquiry (Rs. 8,93,224 and Rs. 4,27,974), economic motivation (33 and 39 score), mass media exposure

(10.25 and 8.00 score), and extension contact (8.25 and 11.00 score) for Haryana and Gujarat States respectively.

Variability in the Socio-personal, Economic and Psychological Characteristics between Management Committee Members of Haryana (N=30) and Gujarat (N=30).

It is evident from Table 5.13 that variability in the mean scores of different management committee member variables was non-significant for majority of the variables and highly significant for few variables.

The variables with non-significant mean score differences were aged 48 and 44 years, total value of assets at the time of inquiry (Rs. 8,15,280 and Rs. 5,33,570), political knowledge and affiliation (12 and 11 score), and mass media exposure (9 and 10 score) for Haryana and Gujarat States respectively. Whereas, the variables with highly significant differences (at 0.01 level of probability) were: commitment towards VMPCS (63 and 71 score) and extension contact (10.0 and 12.5 score) for Haryana and Gujarat States respectively.

Table 5.13. Variability in the Socio-Personal, Economic and Psychological Characteristics between Management Committee Members of Haryana (N=30) and Gujarat (N=30)

S. No.	Traits	Mean Value		't' value
		Haryana	Gujarat	
1.	Age (Years)	48	44	1.125
2.	Total Value of Assets at the time of inquiry (Rs.)	8,15,280	5,33,570	1.488
3.	Commitment towards VMPCS (Score)	63	71	8.983**
4.	Political Knowledge and Affiliation (Score)	12	11	0.797
5.	Mass Media Exposure (Score)	9	10	0.287
6.	Extension Contact (Score)	10.0	12.5	2.751**

** Significant at 0.01 level of probability.

Variability in the Village Infrastructure and VMPCSs Variables between Haryana (N=6) and Gujarat (N=6)

This section has been further sub-divided into following sub-heads:

(1) Variability in village infrastructure and population characteristics.
(2) Variability in milk collection business traits.
(3) Variability in performance traits of VMPCSs.

Variability in Village Infrastructure and Population Characteristics

A perusal of Table 5.14 reflected that majority of the variables (based on '*t*' values) concerning village infrastructure and population characteristics were having non-significant mean score difference and a few were having significant or highly significant mean score difference.

Table 5.14. Variability in the Village Infrastructure and Population Characteristics between Management Committee Members of Haryana and Gujarat

S. No.	Traits	Mean Value		't' value
		Haryana	Gujarat	
1.	Village Infrastructure (%)	58	32	2.340*
2.	Total Agricultural Land per Village (ha)	488	242	1.592
3.	Total Irrigated Land per Village (%)	97	80	1.414
4.	Average Village Population (No.)	3367	1533	1.641
5.	Number of Households per Village	335	306	0.185
6.	Number of Members per Household	10	7	1.849
7.	Joint Families per Village (%)	43	24	1.127
8.	Nuclear Families per Village (%)	57	76	1.115
9.	Percentage of Dominant Caste People per Village	27	65	2.139
10.	Average Literacy Rate per Village (%)	78	65	1.430
11.	Average distance of VMPCS from Chilling Centre (Km)	44	17	6.656**
12.	Average distance of VMPCS from Nearest Milk Plant (Km)	44	20	5.095**

* Significant at 0.05 level of probability.

** Significant at 0.01 level of probability.

The variables having non-significant mean score difference were: total agricultural land per village (488 and 242 hectares), total irrigated land per village (97 and 80%), average village population (3367 and 1533), number of households per village (335 and 306), number of members per household (10 and 7), joint families per village (43 and 24%), nuclear families per village (57 and 76%), percentage of dominant caste people per village (27 and 65), and average literacy rate per village (27 and 65%) for Haryana and Gujarat States, respectively.

Variable having significant (at 0.05 level of probability) mean score difference was: village infrastructure (58 and 32%), and variables having highly significant mean score difference (at 0.01 level of probability) were: average distance of VMPCS from chilling centre (44 and 17 kilometres and average distance of VMPCS from nearest milk plant (44 and 20 kilometres) for Haryana and Gujarat States, respectively.

Variability in Milk Collection Business Traits

It may be visualised from Table 5.15 that mean score difference for milk collection business traits was significant for VMPCSs, and non-significant for vendors, and business by member-farmers directly. The significant (at 0.05 level of probability) mean score difference was observed in case of average daily milk collection business in rupees, per household, by VMPCS, of cow milk (Rs. 0.16 and Rs. 1.14), buffalo milk (Rs. 3.76 and Rs. 18.74), and total milk (Rs. 3.93 and Rs. 19.88) for Haryana and Gujarat States, respectively.

Variability in Performance Traits of VMPCSs

It is apparent from Table 5.16 that the mean score difference values for performance traits of VMPCSs were non-significant for majority of the traits, viz., yearly milk spoilage per VMCPS (1.31 and 0.56%), volume of business per farmer-member per VMPCS per year (Rs. 5,108 and Rs. 6,123),

Table 5.15. Variability in Milk Collection Business Traits between Haryana (N=6) and Gujarat (N=6)

S. No.	Trait		Mean Value		't' value
			Haryana	Gujarat	
1.	Average daily milk collection business in rupees per household by:				
	(a) VMPCS				
		Cow	0.16	1.14	2.513*
		Buffalo	3.76	18.74	2.631*
		Total	3.93	19.88	2.747*
	(b) Vendors				
		Cow	0.31	0.05	1.396
		Buffalo	0.98	1.56	0.772
		Total	1.29	1.61	0.380
	(c) Member-farmers directly in the village				
		Cow	0.08	0.00	1.959
		Buffalo	0.46	0.10	1.449
		Total	0.54	0.10	1.560

* Significant at 0.05 level of probability.

manpower per one lakh rupees business per year per VMPCS (0.78 and 0.44), number of A.I. done per farmer-member per year per VMPCS (3.16 and 0.00), emergency visits per farmer VMPCS (0.34 and 1.18), quantity of fodder seed supplied per farmer-member per year per VMPCS (0.46 and 0.01 kg), tours conducted per year per VMPCS (0.11 and 0.11), cattle shows organised per year per VMPCS (0.05 and 0.00), film shows done per year per VMPCS (0.05 and 0.00), membership performance per VMPCS (15.0 and 15.0), and household coverage performance per VMPCS (11.33 and 17.00) for Haryana and Gujarat States, respectively.

Table 5.16. Variability in Performance Traits of VMPCSs between Haryana (N=6) and Gujarat (N=6)

S. No.	Trait	Mean Value		't' value
		Haryana	Gujarat	
1.	Number of farmer-members per VMPCS	53	206	3.887**
2.	Number of farmer-members actually supplying milk per VMPCS	36	100	2.590*
3.	Yearly milk spoilage per VMPCS (%)	1.31	0.56	1.755
4.	Number of paid employees per farmer-member per VMPCS	0.0273	0.0154	2.839*
5.	Volume of business per farmer-member per VMPCS per year (Rs.)	5108	6123	0.556
6.	Manpower per one lakh rupees business per year per VMPCS	0.78	0.44	1.435
7.	Number of A.I. done per farmer-member per year per VMPCS	3.16	0.00	1.115
8.	Emergency visits per farmer-member per year per VMPCS (No.)	0.34	1.18	1.270
9.	Quantity of cattle feed supplied per farmer-member per year per VMPCS (kg)	76	304	5.384**
10.	Quantity of fodder seed supplied per farmer-member per year per VMPCS (kg)	0.46	0.01	2.073
11.	Tours conducted per year per VMPCS (No.)	0.11	0.11	0.000
12.	Cattle shows conduct per year per VMPCS (No.)	0.05	0.00	1.005
13.	Film show done per year per VMPCS (No.)	0.05	0.00	1.005
14.	Membership performance per VMPCS (Score)	9.50	9.33	0.423
15.	Milk price performance per VMPCS (Score)	37	48	4.445**
16.	Milk collection performance per VMPCS (Score)	15	15	0.000
17.	Household coverage performance per VMPCS (Score)	11.33	17.00	1.503
18.	Overall performance per VMPCS (Score)	74	90	2.328**

* Significant at 0.05 level of probability.

** Significant at 0.01 level of probability.

Whereas, significant (at 0.05 level of probability) differences were observed in the mean scores of traits like: number of farmer members actually supplying milk per VMPCS (36 and 100), number of paid employees per farmer per VMPCS (0.0273 and 0.0154), and overall performance per VMPCS (74 and 90 score) for Haryana and Gujarat States, respectively.

Highly significant (at 0.01 level of probability) mean score differences were observed in traits like, number of farmer members per VMPCS (53 and 206), quantity of cattle feed supplied per farmer member per year per VMPCS (76 and 304 kg), and milk price performance per VMPCS (38 and 48 score) for Haryana and Gujarat States, respectively.

Effect of Different Factors on the Performance of Milk Co-operatives in Haryana and Gujarat

As described earlier (Fig. 5.1) showing performance curves of Haryana and Gujarat States), the Gujarat VMPCSs performed better than Haryana VMPCSs with respect to most of the factors/indicators affecting performance of milk co-operatives. The factors affecting the success of milk co-operatives have been analysed on the basis of comparison of mean score values and estimation of '*t*' values. These factors have been listed in Table 5.17 and presented below under the following sub-heads:

(1) Factors affecting success of milk co-operatives in Gujarat.

(2) Factors contributing to performance of milk co-operatives in Haryana.

These factors have been sub-divided as follows:

(1) Member-farmers traits affecting success of milk co-operatives in Gujarat.

(2) Management committee members traits affecting the success of milk Co-operatives in Gujarat.

(3) Environmental and infrastructural traits affecting the success of milk co-operatives in Gujarat.

(4) Organisational traits affecting the success of milk co-operatives in Gujarat.

Factors affecting Success of Milk Co-operative in Gujarat

Member-Farmers Traits affecting Success of Milk Co-operatives in Gujarat

An analysis of Table 5.17 revealed that the factors crucial for the success of milk co-operative in Gujarat (on the basis of mean scores and '*t*' values) were: higher economic motivation (39 in Gujarat and 33 in Haryana), higher extension contact (11.0 in Gujarat and 8.25 in Haryana), lower milk consumption per household (1.95 litres in Gujarat and 3.81 litres in Haryana), lower value of assets at the time of inquiry (Rs. 4,27,974 in Gujarat and Rs. 8,93,224 in Haryana), and higher milk sale per household (6.41 litres in Gujarat and 4.94 litres in Haryana). Thus, lower value of assets of Gujarat dairy farmers seems to have led to their higher economic motivation and thereby to higher extension contacts in order to produce and sell more milk for higher income.

Management Committee Member Traits affecting the Success of Milk Co-operatives in Gujarat

It may be observed from Table 5.17 that mean scores of the crucial traits for management committee members were higher in Gujarat than in Haryana, viz., higher commitment towards VMPCSs (71 in Gujarat and 63 in Haryana) and higher extension contacts (12.5 in Gujarat and 10.0 in Haryana). Higher commitment and extension contacts of management committee members helped in many ways to improve the organisational effectiveness and efficiency of milk co-operatives leading to better services and higher returns for member-farmers and financial ability of milk co-operatives in Gujarat.

Environmental and Infrastructural Traits affecting the Success of Milk Cooperatives in Gujarat

The results in Table 5.17 indicated that environmental and infrastructural traits affecting success of milk co-operatives in Gujarat were: lower average distance of VMPCs from chilling centre (17 km in Gujarat and 44 km in Haryana), and lower average distance of VMPCS from nearest milk plant (20 km in Gujarat and 44 km in Haryana). These two factors significantly reduced the cost of transportation and milk spoilage in way, leading to improved efficiency of VMPCSs of Gujarat.

Organisational Traits affecting the Success of Milk Co-operatives in Gujarat

It is evident from Table 5.17 that most of the organisational variables affecting success of milk co-operatives were reported significantly better in Gujarat than in Haryana. These factors were: higher quantity of cattle feed supplied per farmer-member per year per VMPCS (304 kg in Gujarat and 76 kg in Haryana), better milk price performance by VMPCS (48 in Gujarat and 38 in Haryana), higher number of farmer-members per VMPCS (206 in Gujarat and 53 in Haryana), lower number of paid employees per farmer-member per VMPCS (0.0154 in Gujarat and 0.0273 in Haryana), higher; average daily milk collection business per household per VMPCS (Rs. 19.88 in Gujarat and Rs. 3.39 in Haryana); higher number of farmer-members actually supplying milk per VMPCS (100 in Gujarat and 36 in Haryana); and higher overall performance score per VMPCS (90 in Gujarat and 74 in Haryana).

Factors Contributing to the Performance of Milk Co-operatives in Haryana

A perusal of Table 5.17 revealed that there were few factors reported significantly better (on the basis of mean scores and

Table 5.17. Factors affecting the Performance of Milk Cooperatives in Gujarat and Haryana

S. No.	Trait	Mean Value		't' value
		Haryana	Gujarat	
1	2	3	4	5
I.	**Member-Farmers' Traits (N=90)**			
1.	Economic motivation (Score)	33	39	9.037**
2.	Extension contact (Score)	8.25	11.00	7.640**
3.	Daily milk consumption per household (litres)	3.81	1.95	5.018**
4.	Total value of assets at the time of inquiry (Rs.)	893224	427974	4.220**
5.	Mass media exposure (Score)	10.25	8.00	3.280**
6.	Daily milk sale per household (litres)	4.94	6.41	2.459*
II.	**Management Committee Members' Traits (N=30)**			
7.	Commitment towards VMPCS (Score)	63	71	8.983**
8.	Extension Contact (Score)	10.0	12.5	2.751**
III.	**Environment and Infrastructural Traits (N=6)**			
9.	Average distance of VMPCS from chilling centre (Km)	44	17	6.656**
10.	Average distance of VMPCS from nearest milk plant (Km)	44	20	5.095**
11.	Village Infrastructure (%)	58	32	2.340**
IV.	**Organizational Traits of VMPCS (N=6)**			
12.	Quantity of cattle feed supplied per farmer-member per year per VMPCS (Kg)	76	304	5.384**
13.	Milk price performance by VMPCS (Score)	38	48	4.445**
14.	Number of farmer-members per VMPCS	53	206	3.887**
15.	Number of paid employees per farmer-member per VMPCS	0.0273	0.0154	2.839**
16.	Average daily milk collection business in rupees, per household per VMPCS	3.93	19.88	2.747**
17.	Number of farmer-members actually supplying milk per VMPCS	36	100	2.590**
18.	Overall performance per VMPCS (Score)	74	90	2.328**

* Significant at 0.05 level of probability.

** Significant at 0.01 level of probability.

'*t*' values) in Haryana in comparison to Gujarat. These factors seem to have contributed significantly and positively to the progress of milk co-operatives in Haryana (in comparison to other States of India with less developed milk co-operatives). These were: higher mass media exposure of member-farmers (10.25 in Haryana and 8.00 in Gujarat), and better village infrastructure (58% in Haryana and 32% in Gujarat). These were the result of advanced agriculture, better facilities and public institution, lower complexity of problems being a small State, awareness of the people and better natural resources in Haryana in comparison to Gujarat. These traits may be exploited effectively to improve the performance of VMPCS in Haryana.

In addition, a few other factors adding to the performance of VMPCS of Haryana were: higher literacy rate of villagers, and better supply of inputs and services like fodder, seed, farmer tours, cattle shows, A.I. etc., provided by VMPCSs and DCMPUs to the farmer-members.

Factors Responsible for Failure of VMPCSs

The factors responsible for failure of VMPCSs (in Haryana, as no VMPCS was reported defunct in the study area of Gujarat) are given in Table 5.18. These factors were based on the perception of members of defunct VMPCSs of Haryana State. These factors in decreasing order or importance were: groupism and casteism in villages (83% response), milk vendors and contractors (75% response), no serious efforts by DCMPU for running newly opened VMPCSs (25% response), disloyalty of member-farmers (21% response), low purchasing power of villagers (13% response) and lack of awareness in villagers (13% response). The other important reasons for failure of VMPCSs in Haryana as observed in the findings were: lower daily milk sale per household, lower economic motivation of member-farmers, lower commitment and extension contacts of management committee members, and lower overall performance of VMPCSs.

Table 5.18. Perceived Reasons for Failure of VMPCSs by Members of Defunct VMPCSs (Haryana State, N=24)

S. No.	Reason	Response Percentage	Rank
I.	**Socio-Personal**		
1.	Groupism and casteism in the villages	83	1
2.	Milk vendors and contractors	75	2
3.	Disloyalty of member-farmers	21	4
II.	**Economic**		
1.	Low purchasing power of villagers	13	6
III.	**Organisational**		
1.	No serious efforts by DCMPU for running new VMPCSs	25	3
IV.	**Psychological**		
1.	Low economic motivation of member-farmers of VMPCSs	17	5
2.	Lack of awareness in villages	13	7

As described in the profile (Table 5.8) of farmer members of defunct VMPCSs of Haryana, their traits like unfavourable attitude towards VMPCSs and lower extension contact does not seem to be responsible for failure of their VMPCSs as these traits were reported similar to those of the member farmers of functional VMPCSs.

Comparative Constraints in the functioning of VMPCSs and DCMPUs

In this section, at attempt was made to enlist and describe various types of constraints in the functioning of VMCPSs and DCMPUs, as perceived by member-farmers of VMPCSs and employees of DCMPUs of Haryana and Gujarat, under the following sub-heads:

(1) Constraints in the functioning of VMPCSs and DCMPUs, as perceived by member-farmers of selected VMPCSs of Haryana (N=90).

(2) Constraints in the functioning of VMPCSs and DCMPUs, as perceived by member-farmers of selected VMPCSs of Gujarat (N=90).

(3) Constraints in the functioning of DCMPUs and VMPCSs, as perceived by employees of selected DCMPUs of Haryana (N=10).
(4) Constraints in the functioning of DCMPUs and VMPCSs, as perceived by employees of selected DCMPUs of Gujarat (N=10).
(5) Comparative constraints in the functioning of VMPCSs and DCMPSs, as perceived by member-farmers of VMPCUs and employees of DCMPUs of Haryana and Gujarat.

Constraints in the functioning of VMPCSs and DCMPUs, as perceived by member-farmers of selected VMPCSs of Haryana (N=90)

This section deals with the description of different types of constraints in the functioning of VMPCSs and DCMPUs as perceived by the member-farmers of selected VMPCSs of Haryana (N=90). These constraints have been further sub-divided into following categories:

(1) Socio-personal constraints
(2) Economic constraints
(3) Organisational constraints
(4) Psychological constraints
(5) Technological constraints

Socio-personal Constraints

Table 5.19 revealed that socio-personal constraints in the functioning of VMPCSs and DCMPUs as perceived by low, medium and high category of milk suppliers in decreasing order of importance were: milk vendors and contractors operating in the village (80% low, 91% medium, 85% high, and 86% overall response), groupism and casteism prevailing in the villages (19% low, 18% medium, 45% high, and 24% overall response), social taboos in milk sale (15% low, 32% medium, 0% high, and 20% overall response), high milk consumption of household (15% low, 9% medium, 0% high, and 9% overall response), misconception that milk sale is a sign of poverty (4% low, 0% medium, 0% high, and 1% overall response), and disloyalty of member-farmers (0% low, 0% medium, 5% high, and 1% overall response). These findings were in line with those of Srivastava (1969), Sohal (1973), Dubey *et al.* (1978), Raju and Maraty (1991) and Singh (1992).

Economic Constraints

The economic constraints as given in Table 5.19 for different categories of respondents were: lower price of milk given by VMPCSs (46% low, 36% medium, 15% high, and 34% overall response), lack of advance facility by VMPCSs (23% low, 39% medium, 25% high, and 31% overall response), lower profitability in dairying (12% low, 32% medium, 40% high, and 28% overall response), high cost of milk production (19% low, 14% medium, 34% high, and 20% overall response), lack of credit facility to poor and needy farmers (15% low, 27% medium, 10% high, and 20% overall response), low purchasing power of villagers (4% low, 2% medium, 10% high, and 4% overall response), and not considering dairying as a business (4% low, 0% medium, 0% high, and 1% overall response). These findings were supported by Dubey *et al.* (1978), Panda (1979), Gopala and Maraty (1989), Shroti (1989) and Aneja (1991).

Organisational Constraints

The findings presented in Table 5.19 indicated that organisational constraints in decreasing order of importance may be enlisted as: lack of efforts towards milk production by VMPCSs and DCMPUs (19% low, 11% medium, 10% high, and 13% overall response), delayed payments by VMPCSs to member-farmers (12% low, 0% medium, 5% high, and 4% overall response), poor quality inputs supplied by VMPCSs and

Table 5.19. Constraints in the functioning of VMPCSs and DCMPUs as perceived by member - farmer of Selected VMPCSs of Haryana (N=90)

S. No.	Constraints	Response Percentage Category of Milk Supplier				Rank Category	Overall
		Low N=26	Medium N=44	High N=20	Overall N=90		
1	2	3	4	5	6	7	8
I.	**Socio-Personal:**						
1.	Milk vendors and contractors operating in the village	80	91	85	86	I	1
2.	Groupism and casteism prevailing in the village	19	18	45	24	II	5
3.	Social taboos in milk sale	15	32	0	20	III	6
4.	High milk consumption of household	15	9	0	9	IV	11
5.	Misconception that milk sale is a sign of poverty	4	0	0	1	V	20
6.	Disloyalty of member-farmers	0	0	5	1	VI	21
II.	**Economical:**						
1.	Lower price of milk given by VMPCS	46	36	15	34	I	2
2.	Lack of advance facility by VMPCS	23	39	25	31	II	3
3.	Lower profitability in dairying	12	32	40	28	III	4
4.	High cost of milk production	19	14	35	20	IV	7

(Contd.)

Table 5.19 (*Contd.*)

1	2	3	4	5	6	7	8
5.	Lack of credit facility to poor and needy farmers	15	27	10	20	V	8
6.	Low purchasing power of villagers	4	2	10	4	VI	12
7.	Not considering dairying as a business	4	0	0	1	VII	22
III.	**Organizational:**						
1.	Lack of efforts towards milk production by VMPCS and DCMPU	19	11	10	13	I	9
2.	Delayed payments by VMPCS to member-farmers	12	0	5	4	II	13
3.	Poor quality inputs supplied by VMPCS	4	0	10	3	III	14
4.	Disloyal contract drivers of milk vans of DCMPU	4	0	0	1	IV	23
IV.	**Psychological:**						
1.	Low economic motivation of member-farmers	12	11	5	10	I	10
2.	Lack of job satisfaction and job security to secretaries of VMPCS	8	2	0	3	II	15
3.	Lack of motivation to secretaries of VMPCS	4	2	0	2	III	17
4.	Ignorance of member-farmers about benefits of joining VMPCS	0	5	0	2	IV	18
5.	Low risk bearing ability of dairy farmers	0	2	0	1	V	24
V.	**Technological:**						
1.	Seasonal variations in milk production	4	0	10	3	I	16
2.	Unreliable fat testing method of VMPCS	8	0	0	2	II	19

DCMPUs (4% low, 0% medium, 10% high, and 3% overall response) and disloyal contract drivers of milk vans of DCMPUs (4% low, 0% medium, 0% high, and 1% overall response). These findings were similar to those of Saini (1975), Dubey *et al.* (1978), Raju and Maraty (1989) and Shroti (1989).

Psychological Constraints

Psychological constraints (Table 5.19) in decreasing order of importance were: low economic motivation of member-farmers (12% low, 11% medium, 5% high, and 10% overall response), lack of job satisfaction and job security to secretaries of VMPCSs (8% low, 2% medium, 0% high, and 3% overall response), lack of motivation to secretaries of VMPCSs (4% low, 2% medium, 0% high, and 2% overall response), ignorance of member-farmers about benefits of joining VMPCSs (0% low, 5% medium, 0% high, and 2% overall response) and low risk bearing ability of dairy farmers (0% low, 2% medium, 0% high, and 1% overall response). These findings were in line with those of Jha (1984) and Raju and Maraty (1991).

Technological Constraints

As given in Table 5.19, the perceived technological constraints for different categories of respondents were: seasonal variations in milk production (4% low, 0% medium, 10% high, and 3% overall response), and unreliable fat testing method of VMPCSs (8% low, 0% medium, 0% high, and 2% overall response). These findings were supported by Singh (1992).

Constraints in the functioning of VMPCSs and DCMPUs, as perceived by Member-Farmers of Selected VMPCSs of Gujarat (N=90)

This section describes different types of constraints in the functioning of VMPCSs and DCMPUs as perceived by member-farmers of selected VMPCSs of Gujarat (N=90).

They have been further sub-divided into following categories:

(1) Socio-personal constraints
(2) Economical constraints
(3) Organisational constraints
(4) Psychological constraints
(5) Technological constraints

Socio-Personal Constraints

Table 5.20 indicated that socio-personal constraints in decreasing order of importance and rank for different categories of milk suppliers were: groupism and casteism prevailing in the villages (65% low, 55% medium, 46% high, and 56% overall response), and milk vendors and contractors operating in the villages (45% low, 52% medium, 36% high, and 44% overall response). These findings were in line with those of Saini (1975), UN/FAO (1981), Mitra (1990) and Singh (1992).

Economical Constraints

As listed in Table 5.20, economical constraints in decreasing order of importance were: scarcity of drinking water for animals (45% low, 52% medium, 57% high, and 51% overall response), scarcity of green fodder for animals (45% low, 32% medium, 29% high, and 36% overall response), shortage of electricity in villages (26% low, 19% medium, 32% high, and 26% overall response), poor village approach roads (29% low, 16% medium, 32% high, and 26% overall response), lack of loaning agency in the villages (26% low, 10% medium, 11% high, and 9% overall response), lower prices of milk given by VMPCSs to the member-farmers (16% low, 13% medium, 4% high, and 3% overall response), scarcity of labour for dairying (0% low, 0% medium, 7% high, and 2% overall response), and low fertility of agricultural land (3% low, 3% medium, 0% high, and 2% overall response). These findings were similar to those of Dubey *et al.* (1978), Jain (1979), Pandey (1981), Nataraju and Chanegowda (1987) and Gopala and Maraty (1989).

Organisational Constraints

The results given in Table 5.20 indicated that organisational constraints for different categories of milk suppliers were: delayed veterinary aid in villages by DCMPUs (3% low, 10% medium, 7% high, and 7% overall response), and lack of efforts towards milk production by DCMPUs and VMPCSs (3% low, 6% medium, 0% high, and 3% overall response). The findings resembled to Dubey *et al.* (1978), Dabas (1984), Raju and Maraty (1991) and Singh (1992).

Psychological Constraints

Psychological constraints in Table 5.20 for different categories of milk suppliers were: low risk bearing ability of dairy farmers (26% low, 16% medium, 32% high, and 24% overall response), negative attitude of member farmers towards A.I. (0% low, 3% medium, 4% high, and 2% overall response), and lack of motivation to secretaries of VMPSs (0% low, 3% medium, 0% high, and 1% overall response). These findings were supported by Raju and Maraty (1991).

Technological Constraints

The only technological constraints (Table 5.20) for different categories of milk suppliers was seasonal variation in milk procurement and production (0% low, 3% medium, 4% high, and 2% overall response). This finding was in line with Singh (1992).

Constraints in the Functioning of DCMPUs and VMPCSs, as Perceived by Employees of Selected DCMPU of Haryana (N=10)

The constraints as perceived by DCMPU employees of Haryana have been further sub-divided into following categories:

(1) Socio-personal constraints
(2) Economical constraints

Table : 5.20. Constraints in the functioning of VMPCSs and DCMPUs as perceived by the member-farmers of VMCSs of Gujarat (N = 90)

S. No.	Constraints	Response Percentage Category of Milk Supplier				Rank Category	Overall
		Low N=26	Medium N=44	High N=20	Overall N=90		
1	2	3	4	5	6	7	8
I.	**Socio-Personal:**						
1.	Groupism and casteism prevailing in the villages	65	55	46	56	I	1
2.	Milk vendors and contractors operating in the village	45	52	36	44	II	3
3.	Disloyalty of member-farmers	6	3	4	4	III	10
II.	**Economical**						
1.	Scarcity of drinking water for animals	45	52	57	51	I	2
2.	Scarcity of green fodder for animals	45	32	29	36	II	4
3.	Shortage of electricity in villages	26	19	32	26	III	5
4.	Poor village approach roads	29	16	32	26	IV	6
5.	Lack of credit facility to poor and needy farmers	26	10	11	9	V	8
6.	Lower price of milk given by VMPCS to the member-farmers	16	13	4	4	VI	11

(*Contd.*)

Table 5.20 (*Contd.*)

1	2	3	4	5	6	7	8
7.	Smaller land holdings	0	6	4	3	VII	12
8.	Scarcity of labour for dairying	0	0	7	2	VIII	14
9.	Lower fertility of agricultural land	3	3	0	2	IX	15
III.	**Organizational**						
1.	Delayed veterinary aid in villages by DCMPU	3	10	7	7	I	9
2.	Lack of efforts towards milk production by VMPCS and DCMPU	3	6	0	3	II	13
IV.	**Psychological**						
1.	Low risk bearing ability of dairy farmers	26	16	32	24	I	7
2.	Negative attitude of farmers towards A.I.	0	3	4	2	II	16
3.	Lack of motivation to secretaries of VMPCS	0	3	0	1	III	18
V.	**Technological**						
	Seasonal variations in milk production and procurement	0	3	4	2	I	17

(3) Organisational constraints
(4) Psychological constraints
(5) Technological constraints

Socio-Personal Constraints

The findings of Table 5.21 revealed that the socio-personal constraints, as perceived by the DCMPU employees, in decreasing order of importance and rank were: farmers do not consider DCMPU as their own and show concern only to the price of milk (10% response), and lack of co-operative spirit among villagers (10% response). It might be due to the non-awareness of the member-farmers about benefits of joining milk co-operatives, and low priority given to co-operative dairying by them.

Economical Constraints

Economic constraints (Table 5.21) in decreasing order of importance were: lower price of milk given by VMPCSs to member farmers (50% response), and lack of working capital with DCMPUs (10% response). The findings were in line with those of Dubey *et al.* (1978), Shroti (1989) and Singh (1992).

Organisational Constraints

Organisational constraints, as listed in Table 5.21, in decreasing order of importance were: differences in policies at DCMPU and VMPCS levels (40% response), vital decisions for milk and milk product prices are reserved for milk federation (40% response), political interference in the working of DCMPUs (30% response), lack of extension activities by DCMPUs (30% response), lack of efforts towards milk production by DCMPUs and VMPCSs (20% response), initiative for starting VMPCS is mainly the responsibility of DCMPUs (20% response), lack of experienced and trained staff at field level (10% response), poor quality of supplies and services by DCMPUs to VMPCSs (10% response), recruitment of DCMPU employees on the basis of availability with the federation and not according to needs of the DCMPU (10% response), disloyal contract drivers of milk vans appointed by DCMPU (10% response), lack of veterinary and insurance facilities to members of VMPCSs (10% response), frequent transfers of DCMPU employees (10% response), frequently changing policies at DCMPU level (10% response), and lower efficiency of co-operative milk plants (10% response). These findings were supported by Bavisekar (1968), Dubey *et al.* (1978). UN/FAO (1981), Raju and Maraty (1991) and Singh (1992).

Psychological Constraints

According to Table 5.21, the psychological constraints in decreasing order of importance were: lack of motivation to DCMPU employees (20% response), lack of motivation to low milk producers (10% response), and lack of knowledge about clean milk production by member-farmers (10% response). These findings were similar to those of Raju and Maraty (1991).

Technological Constraints

Only technological constraint reported (Table 5.21), was seasonal variation in the production and procurement of milk (10% response). This finding was supported by Singh (1992).

Constraints in the Functioning of DCMPUs and VMPCSs, as Perceived by Employees of Selected DCMPUs of Gujarat (N=10)

Perceived constraints in the functioning of VMPCSs and DCMPUs have been further sub-divided into following categories:

Table 5.21. Constraints in the functioning of DCMPUs and VMPCSs as Perceived by Selected Employees of DCMPU of Haryana (N=10)

S. No.	Constraints	Response Percentage	Rank	
			Category	Overall
1	2	3	4	5
I.	**Socio-Personal:**			
1.	Farmers do not consider DCMPU as their own and show concern only to the price of milk	10	I	9
2.	Lack of co-operative spirit among villagers	10	II	10
II.	**Economic:**			
1.	Lower price of milk given by VMPCS to member-farmers	50	I	1
2.	Lack of working capital with DCMPU	10	II	11
III.	**Organizational:**			
1.	Differences in policies at DCMPU and VMPCS levels	40	I	2
2.	Vital decisions for milk and milk product prices are reserved for milk federation	40	II	3
3.	Political interference in the working of DCMPU	30	III	4
4.	Lack of extension activities by DCMPU	30	IV	5
5.	Lack of efforts towards milk production by DCMPU and VMPS	20	V	6
6.	Initiative for starting VMPCS is the responsibility of DCMPU mainly	20	VI	7
7.	Lack of experienced and trained staff at field level	10	VII	12
8.	Poor quality of supplies and services provided by DCMPU to VMPCS	10	VIII	13
9.	Recruitment of DCMPU employees on the basis of availability with the federation and not according to need of DCMPU	10	IX	14
10.	Disloyal contract drivers of milk vans appointed by DCMPU	10	X	15
11.	Lack of veterinary and insurance facilities to members of VMPCS	10	XI	16

(*Contd.*)

Table 5.21 (*Contd.*)

1	2	3	4	5
12.	Frequent transfers of DCMPU employees	10	XII	17
13.	Frequently changing policies at DCMPU level	10	XIII	18
14.	Lower efficiency of co-operative milk plants	10	XIV	19
IV.	**Psychological:**			
1.	Lack of motivation to DCMPU employees	20	I	8
2.	Lack of motivation to low milk producers	10	II	20
3.	Lack of knowledge about clean milk production by member-farmers	10	III	21
V.	**Technological:**			
	Seasonal variations in production and procurement of milk	10	I	22

(1) Socio-personal constraints
(2) Economical constraints
(3) Organisational constraints
(4) Psychological constraints
(5) Technological constraints

Socio-Personal Constraints

The findings of Table 5.22 indicated that socio-personal constraints in decreasing order of importance were: groupism and casteism at VMPCS level (90% response), and milk vendors and contractors operating in the villages (60% response). These findings were supported by Sohal (1973), Dubey *et al.* (1978), Gurucharan and Degra (1984), Dabas (1984) and Singh (1992).

Economical Constraints

As listed in Table 5.22, the important economic constraints were: scarcity of green fodder for animals (40% response), low purchasing power of villages (30% response), poor condition of village approach roads (20% response), scarcity of drinking water for animals (20% response), and lower fertility of agricultural lands (10% response). These findings were in line with those of Patel *et al.* (1975) and Nataraju and Channegowda (1987).

Organisational Constraints

Table 5.22 indicated that organisational constraints in decreasing order of importance were: overstaffing at DCMPU level (10% response), and lack of efforts towards milk production by DCMPUs and VMPCs (10% response). These findings were similar to Dubey *et al.* (1978), Dabas (1984) and Mescarneshas (1988).

Psychological Constraints

As depicted in Table 5.22, psychological constraints in decreasing order of importance were: lack of motivation (10% response), and lack of job satisfaction to DCMPU employees (10% response). These findings were supported by Raju and Maraty (1991).

Technological Constraints

The technological constraint, as given in Table 5.22 was: seasonal variation in milk production and procurement (20% response). This finding was supported by Singh (1992).

Comparative Constraints in the Functioning of VMPCSs and DCMPUs as Perceived by Member-Farmers of VMPCSs and Employees of DCMPUSs of Haryana and Gujarat

The constraints have been compared on the basis of commonness between Haryana and Gujarat States under the following sub-heads:

(1) Common constraints in the functioning of VMPCSs and DCMPUs as perceived by member-farmers of Haryana (N=90) and Gujarat (N=90).

Table 5.22. Constraints in the Functioning of DCMPUs and VMPCSs as Perceived by Selected Employees of DCMPU of Gujarat (N=10)

S. No.	Constraints	Response Percentage	Rank	
			Category	Overall
I.	**Socio-Personal:**			
1.	Groupism and casteism prevailing in the villages	90	I	1
2.	Milk vendors and contractors operating in the villages	60	II	2
II.	**Economical:**			
1.	Scarcity of green fodder for animals	40	I	3
2.	Low purchasing power of villagers	30	II	4
3.	Poor condition of village approach roads	20	III	5
4.	Scarcity of drinking water for animals	20	IV	6
5.	Lower fertility of agricultural lands	10	V	8
III.	**Organizational:**			
1.	Overstaffing at DCMPU level	10	I	9
2.	Lack of efforts towards milk production by DCMPU and VMPCS	10	II	10
IV.	**Psychological:**			
1.	Lack of motivation to DCMPU employees	10	I	11
2.	Lack of job satisfaction to DCMPU employees	10	II	12
V.	**Technological:**			
	Seasonal variations in milk production and procurement	20	I	7

(2) Common constraints in the functioning of DCMPUs and VMPCSs as perceived by employees of DCMPUs of Haryana (N=10) and Gujarat (N=10).

(3) Uncommon constraints in the functioning of VMPCSs and DCMPUs as perceived by member-farmers of Haryana (N=90) and Gujarat (N=90).

(4) Uncommon constraints in the functioning of DCMPUs and VMPCSs as perceived by employees of DCMPUs of Haryana (N=10) and Gujarat (N=10).

Common Constraints in the functioning of VMPCSs and DCMPUSs as Perceived by Member-Farmers of Haryana (N=90) and Gujarat (N=90)

As presented in Table 5.23, common constraints perceived by member farmers in Haryana and Gujarat were: milk vendors and contractors operating in the village (1st and 3rd rank), lower price of milk given by VMPCS (2nd and 11th rank), groupism and casteism prevailing in the village (5th and 1st rank), lack of credit facility to poor and needy farmers (8th and 8th rank), lack of efforts towards milk production by VMPCS (9th and 13th rank), disloyalty of member farmers (21st and 10th rank) and low risk bearing ability of dairy farmers (24th and 7th rank). Milk vendors and contractors operating in the village, groupism and casteism prevailing in the village were given importance by member farmers of both the states. Thus, socio-personal constraints were given high weightage in both the states. Psychological constraints in Haryana and organisational constraints in Gujarat were given low weightage by the member farmers of VMPCs of the two states.

Common constraints in the functioning of DCMPUs and VMPCSs as Perceived by Employees of DCMPUs of Haryana (N=10) and Gujarat (N=10)

Owing to different socio-economic conditions and different developmental stages of milk co-operatives, very few constraints were reported common (Table 5.24) in the two states. They were, lack of efforts towards milk production by DCMPU and VMPFS (6th and 10th rank), lack of motivation to DCMPU employees (8th and 11th rank), and seasonal variations in milk production and procurement (22nd and 7th rank) for Haryana and Gujarat states, respectively. Thus, employees of milk unions of both the states emphasised organisational and psychological constraints more than any other type of constraints.

Table 5.23. Common Constraints in the functioning of VMPCSs and DCMPUs as perceived by Member-Farmers of Haryana (N=90) and Gujarat (N=90)

S. No.	Constraints	Rank	
		Haryana	Gujarat
1.	Milk vendors and contractors operating in the village	1	3
2.	Lower price of milk given by VMPCS	2	11
3.	Groupism and casteism prevailing in the village	5	1
4.	Lack of credit facility to poor and needy farmers	8	8
5.	Lack of efforts towards milk production by VMPCS and DCMPU	9	13
6.	Disloyalty of member-farmers	21	10
7.	Low risk bearing ability of dairy farmers	24	7

Uncommon Constraints in the functioning of VMPCSs and DCMPUs as perceived by Member Farmers of Haryana (N=90) and Gujarat (N=90)

There were many dissimilar constraints in the two states (Tablc 5.24). Among them few important constraints as perceived by member farmers of Haryana were: lack of advance facility by VMPCS (3rd rank), lower profitability

Table 5.24. Common Constraints in the functioning of VMPCSs and DCMPUs as perceived by Employees of DCMPUs of Haryana (N=90) and Gujarat (N=90)

S. No.	Constraints	Rank	
		Haryana	Gujarat
1.	Lack of efforts towards milk production by DCMPU and VMPCS	6	10
2.	Lack of motivation to DCMPU employees	8	11
3.	Seasonal variations in milk production and procurement	22	7

in dairying (4th rank) and social taboos in milk sale (6th rank). However, Gujarat farmers perceived scarcity of drinking water for animals (2nd rank), scarcity of green fodder for animals (4th rank), and shortage of electricity in villages (5th rank) as the major constraints. Economic constraints were given more importance in Haryana as well as in Gujarat but they were of different nature in the two States.

Uncommon Constraints in the Functioning of DCMPUs and VMPCSs as Perceived by Employees of DCMPUs of Haryana (N=90) and Gujarat (N=90)

An analysis of revealed that constraints perceived to be important by DCMPU employees of Haryana were: lower price of milk given by VMPCSs (1st rank), and differences in policies at DCMPU and VMPCS levels (2nd rank). Whereas, Gujarat employees of DCMPU perceived groupism and casteism in villages (1st rank) and milk vendors and contractors operating in the villages (2nd rank) as the serious constraints. Haryana employees gave more weightage to economic and organisational constraints, whereas, Gujarat employees gave more weightage to socio-personal constraints.

Summary and Implications

In this section, an attempt has been made to highlight the salient findings of the study, and implications drawn thereupon. India is predominantly an agrarian country. Its economy is based on agriculture, of which dairying is a significant component. Dairy development fits most appropriately to the country's programme of increasing food production and employment in rural areas. Here, dairying like all other agricultural enterprises rests with the individual units of small size. Most of the farmers belong to the small or marginal category, owning two to three cattle and less than two hectares of land. These farmers are scattered all over the country and are vulnerable to a variety of factors peculiar to the dairy industry.

The marketing of milk produced by these dairy farmers depends upon three major outlets, viz., milk vendors, private milk plants, and milk co-operatives. The first two sources have been perceived to be exploitative by the dairy farmers. The third outlet (milk co-operative) for milk is least exploitative and organised by the producers themselves (Singh, 1992). Its real significance was understood only when the integrated system of dairy co-operatives was evolved at Anand (Gujarat) and then extended to other parts of the country.

The decision to transfer the Anand type dairy co-operatives to other parts of India was in fact a recognition of the importance of some of the lessons learnt at Anand. The people involved and the situations cannot be recreated as each setting will be unique, but what remains is the concept of the milk co-operatives and how it can be transplanted to other regions. In transferring the concept under OF-I and OF - II, a core group of people who have been trained at Anand have formed a nucleus for transferring Anand Type VMPCSs to whole country.

The National Commission on Agriculture (1976) indicated that most of the co-operatives have failed to develop properly. Doubts have been expressed about the efficacy of co-operative structure for development of dairying in the country. This has happened despite the fact that in most of the developed countries, dairying is based on co-operative organisations. Sidhu and Sidhu (1990) revealed that "Anand Pattern" which was highly successful in Gujarat State, when introduced in Punjab had not proved to be very successful due to different socio-economic conditions of the two States.

Some of the studies on milk co-operatives like Patel (1980), Bhanja (1981), Gopal (1983), Dabas (1984), Singh (1987) and Singh (1992) reported that milk co-operatives have done remarkably well in Gujarat (6.5% of total milk production in 1989-90). However, milk co-operatives could not prove their mettle in many other States of the country, especially in major milk producing States like, Uttar Pradesh

(17.8% of total milk production in 1989-90), Punjab (9.7% of total milk production in 1989-90), and Haryana (6.1% of total milk production in 1989-90). Their poor performance in these States could be attributed to various factors such as: irregular payments, malpractices of secretary of VMPCS, lack of technical persons, competition by vendors, political interference, and unconducive socio-personal, economic, psychological, organisational and environmental factors etc. Similarly, the good performance of milk co-operatives in States like Gujarat might be due to some other factors which needed to be ascertained and validated. So, in order to answer the queries related to the performance of milk co-operatives, the present study entitled *Performance of Milk Co-operatives in Haryana and Gujarat — A Comparative Study* was conducted and the summary of the results have been given below.

The study was conducted in purposively selected States of Gujarat and Haryana. Being the pioneer in milk co-operative sector Gujarat State was selected and Haryana representing a State with high milk production potential, but where milk co-operatives are said to be not working well.

Salient Findings

Comparative Profile of the Member-Farmers of VMPCSs of Haryana and Gujarat

Most of the members in both the States were of middle age (30-56 years), having medium herd size (2-8 animals), producing 3.5 to 14 litres, consuming 0.25 to 5.5 litres, and selling 1.75 to 9.75 litres medium quantities of milk per day. Most of them were having medium value of assets (between Rs. 3,90,740 and Rs. 9,88,565); economic motivation (30 to 40 score) and possessing neutral attitude (21 to 35 score) towards VMPCS, exposed to medium (5 to 14 score) extent of mass media, and having medium (7 to 13 score) extension contacts.

Comparative Profile of the Management Committee Members of Haryana and Gujarat

Major portion of the management committee members in Haryana as well as in Gujarat were possessing characters like, middle age, medium valued assets, medium level of commitment (61 to 72 score) towards VMPCSs, medium political knowledge and affiliation (8 to 15 score), medium mass-media exposure and medium extension contacts.

Comparative Performance Index of Haryana and Gujarat

Mean performance of selected VMPCSs was 60.29 per cent in Haryana and 72.62 per cent in Gujarat, and the overall average was 66.45 per cent. Thus, Gujarat VMPCSs performed significantly better (12.33% higher) than Haryana VMPCSs.

Comparative Variability of Different Traits affecting Performance of VMPCSs in Haryana and Gujarat

Variability in the Member Farmers' Traits

Member farmers' traits varying significantly between Haryana and Gujarat, were: daily milk consumption per household (3.81 and 1.95 litres), total value of assets at the time of inquiry (Rs. 8,93,224 and Rs. 4,27,974), economic motivation (33 and 39 score), mass media exposure (at 5 per cent level of probability), and daily milk sale per household (4.94 and 6.41 litres, at 1 per cent level of probability).

Variability in the Management Committee Members' Traits

Most of these traits were found to be varying non- significantly. A few traits varying significantly (at 1% level of probability) were: commitment towards VMPCS (63 and 71 score) and extension contact (10.0 and 12.50 score) for Haryana and Gujarat States, respectively.

Variability in Village Infrastructure and VMPCS Variables

Majority of the variables under study, concerning village

infrastructure and VMPCS were having non-significant variability between Haryana and Gujarat States. The variables showing significant mean difference between Haryana and Gujarat were: village infrastructure (58% and 32%), average distance from chilling centre (44 and 17 km.), average distance of VMPCS from nearest milk plant (44 and 20 km.), average daily milk collection business per household per VMPCS (Rs. 3.93 and Rs. 19.88), number of farmer-members per VMPCS (53 and 206), number of farmer-members actually supplying milk per VMPCS (36 and 100), number of paid employees per farmer-member per VMPCS (0.0273 and 0.0154), quantity of cattle feed supplied per farmer-member per VMPCS (76 and 304 kg), milk price performance per VMPCS (38 and 48 score) and overall performance per VMPCS (74 and 90 score).

Factors affecting Success of VMPCs

Member-Farmers Traits affecting Success of VMPCSs

Out of the various traits studied, a few reported to affect the success of VMPCSs were: higher economic motivation, higher extension contact, lower milk consumption per household, lower value of assets, and higher milk sale per household.

Management Committee Members' Traits affecting the Success of VMPCSs

Management Committee Members used to be the leaders of the VMPCSs. So, only a few crucial traits were studied. The traits found to affect the success of VMPCSs were: higher commitment towards VMPCSs, and higher extension contacts of management committee members.

Environmental and Infrastructural Traits affecting Success of VMPCSs

Environmental and infrastructural traits reported to affect the success of VMPCSs were: lower average distance of VMPCSs from chilling centre, and lower average distance of VMPCS from milk plant.

Organisational Traits affecting Success of VMPCSs

These traits were related to the various activities and overall performance of VMPCSs. The organisational traits affecting success of VMPCSs were: higher quantity of cattle feed supply, better milk price performance of VMPCSs, higher number of registered member-farmers, lower number of paid employees, higher daily milk collection business, higher number of members supplying milk to VMPCS, and better overall performance of VMPCS.

Factors Responsible for Failure of VMPCSs

The study brought out some important (based upon percentage of response) factors responsible for the failure of VMPCS. They were, groupism and casteism in villages (83%), milk vendors and contractors (75%), no serious efforts by DCMPU for running newly opened VMPCSs (25%), disloyalty of member-farmers (21%), low economic motivation level of member-farmers (17%), low purchasing power of villagers (13%), and lack of awareness in villagers (13%). The other important factors responsible for failure of VMPCSs in Haryana were: lower daily milk sale per household, lower economic motivation of member-farmers, lower commitment, extension contacts of management committee members, and lower overall performance of VMPCSs.

Constraints in the Functioning of VMPCSs and DCMPUs

Constraints Perceived by Farmer-Members of VMPCSs

Serious constraints (on the basis of rank order analysis) as perceived by member-farmers of VMPCSs of Haryana were: milk vendors and contractors, lower price of milk given by VMPCSs, lack of efforts towards milk production by VMPCSs and low economic motivation of member-farmers. The constraints perceived by Gujarat member-farmers were: groupism and casteism prevailing in villages, scarcity of water and green fodder in the villages, low risk bearing ability of dairy farmers, and delayed veterinary aid by DCMPU.

Constraints as Perceived by Employees of DCMPUs

As described by the employees of selected DCMPUs of Haryana, important constraints (on the basis of rank order analysis) in the functioning of VMPCSs and DCMPUs were: lower price of milk given by VMPCSs, differences in policies at DCMPU and VMPCS levels, vital decisions for milk and milk product prices reserved by milk federation, lack of motivation to DCMPU employees, and farmers not considering DCMPU as their own and showing concern only to the price of milk. Whereas, constraints perceived by DCMPU employees of Gujarat were of somewhat different kind, viz., groupism and casteism at VMPCS level, scarcity of green fodder in villages, seasonal variations in milk production and procurement, overstaffing at DCMPU level and lack of motivation to DCMPU employees.

Implications

The findings of the present investigation in relation to the performance of VMPCSs have great practical implications in view of the national policy to promote milk co-operatives in India. Some of the implications of this study have been enumerated as under:

— This study clearly brought about four indicators of performance of VMPCSs on which the VMPCSs were graded initially. These indicators may be useful in evaluating the VMPCSs of various States and formulating future course of action to bring the performance to a desired level.

— The study brings into limelight some of the important traits of member-farmers and management committee members of successful VMPCSs, viz., aged and matured members, lower milk consumption, higher milk sale, higher economic motivation, positive attitude towards VMPCSs, and higher mass media exposure of the member-farmers, and higher commitment, higher political knowledge and affiliation, higher mass media exposure and higher extension contact of management committee members. The analysis of such traits may help the planners to evaluate the performance of VMPCSs and undertake measures to improve their performance.

— Present study compared infrastructural and organisational traits of VMPCSs of successful and unsuccessful VMPCSs. This type of comparison may be helpful for the bureaucrats and leaders to understand the core of success and thus to draw a realistic and feasible plan for the replication of "Anand Pattern" VMPCSs in other States of India.

— The study revealed manpower to be a significant factor for the success of VMPCSs. Thus, it is to be seen carefully by the organisers that VMPCSs are not unnecessarily overburdened with manpower which would only increase the manifold expenditure at the cost of development of VMPCS. VMPCSs should also undertake business other than milk marketing to the advantage of the members. This would aid to the income of VMPCS and provide adequate work to the under-utilized staff.

— Managing committee members with larger land holding and higher value of assets were observed to be less effective which indicated that better-off families in village get into management committee as a prestige symbol without any serious interest in the VMPCS affairs. Thus, care should be taken in choosing managing committee members preferably of small land holding, with larger family size, and who have greater dependency on dairying. Such leaders would take more of genuine interest in VMPCS affairs.

— Economic motivation, extension contact, commitment towards VMPCSs, distance from chilling centre and milk plant, quantity of cattle feed supply, daily milk collection business, milk price, performance of VMPCSs etc., were some of the crucial factors for the success of VMPCSs. It is important to study these factors before starting new VMPCSs at any place.

— In order to economise the time, efforts and money, organisation of VMPCSs must be judged against agricultural resources and village infrastructure at the command of a village, before formulating policies at higher levels for replication of "Anand Pattern" VMPCSs.

— This study enumerated factors responsible for failure of VMPCSs in an otherwise potential State like Haryana, viz., groupism and casteism in villages, milk vendors and contractors, disloyalty of member farmers, low purchasing power of villagers, no serious efforts by DCMPU for running new VMPCSs, low economic motivation of member-farmers and lack of awareness in villagers etc. Corrective measures should be undertaken at DCMPU and Milk Federation levels, by higher officials in order to reduce and finally eliminate these drawbacks from milk co-operatives.

— The study indicated about various constraints perceived by member-farmers of a developed and an under-developed State with respect to milk co-operatives, e.g., milk vendors and contractors, lack of efforts towards milk production by VMPCSs and DCMPUs, low economic motivation of member-farmers, groupism and casteism in villages, scarcity of water and green fodder, lower risk bearing ability of dairy farmers, and delayed veterinary aid by DCMPUs. If the bureaucrats and higher level managers honestly try to reduce these constraints then the performance of VMPCSs in different States of India may be improved significantly in near future. This will definitely improve the income levels of poor dairy farmers in the country.

— This study delineated serious constraints perceived by employees of DCMPUs, like, difference in policies at DCMPU and VMPCS levels, vital decisions for milk and milk product prices reserved for milk federation officials, lack of motivation to employees of DCMPU, seasonal variations in production and procurement of milk, etc. In order to remove these bottlenecks, better co-ordination, decentralised decision making, provision of rewards on the basis of performance, and flexibility in the working of milk plants etc. must be incorporated in the bye-laws in order to make these co-operatives viable and efficient and to be able to compete with private milk industry.

References

Acharya, K.T. and Huria, V.K. (1986). Rural Poverty and Operation Flood. *Economic and Political Weekly*, 21: 37 (13 Sept., 1986) : 1651-1653.

Aneja, R.P. (1991). Indian Dairying - Opportunities and Challenges, 24th Dairy Industry Conference, New Delhi.

Anonymous (1987). *Dairy India*, Rekha Printers Pvt. Ltd., New Delhi.

Anonymous (1992). *Dairy India*, Rekha Printers Pvt. Ltd., New Delhi.

Baviskar, B.S. (1968). Co-operation and Politics, *Economic and Political Weekly*, 3:(12) : 490.

Baviskar, B.S. (1980). *The Politics of Development : Sugar Co-operatives in Rural Maharashtra.* Oxford University Press, Delhi.

Baviskar, B.S. (1986). Dairy Development in a Tribal Area of Gujarat. Working Papers, Dairy Aid and Development, Institute of Social Studies, The Hague.

Baviskar, B.S. (1990). Dairy co-operatives and rural development in Gujarat. In : M. Doornbos and K.N. Nair (Eds.). *Resources, Institutions and Strategies : Operation Flood and Indian Dairying*, New Delhi, Sage Publications.

Baviskar, B.S. and Terhal, P. (1990). Internal constraints and external dependence : EEC and Operation Flood. In : M. Doornbos and K.N. Nair (eds.). *Resources, Institutions and Strategies : Operation Flood and Indian Dairying*, New Delhi, Sage Publications.

Bhanja, S.K. (1981). "A study of socio-economic and psychological correlates in organisation and functioning of dairy co-operatives." Unpublished Ph.D. Thesis, Kurukshetra University, Kurukshetra.

Bhatnagar, O.P. (1974). Constraints to the differential acceptance of the components of new agricultural technology. In : Singh, D. and Pandey, J.S. (eds.). *Transfer of Technology System and Constraints*. Pub. "Nirbal-Ke-Balram", Kanpur.

Bhople, R.S. and Agrawal, S.S. (1987). Constraints in adoption of farm technology. Paper presented in the Seminar on Constraints in TOT held at KKV, Dapoli, Oct. 20-30, 1987.

Bora, P.C. (1990). Use of Agricultural Technology, *The Assam Tribune*, Feb. 9, p. 5.

Brown, E.J. and Bealer, R.C. 1975. Value orientation and behavioural correlates of members in purchasing co-operatives. *Rural Sociology*, 22(1) : 50.

Chaterjee, D.N. (1966). A study of multipurpose co-operative societies and factors associated with their functioning, Kanjhawala Block, Delhi. Unpublished M.Sc. Thesis, IARI, New Delhi.

Chaubey, K.N. (1991). A study on the differential rationality in decision-making among dairy farmers in relation to dairy innovation in Allahabad district (U.P.). Unpublished Ph.D. Thesis, N.D.R.I., Karnal.

Chothani, A.A.; Thakur, D.S.; and Nanda, S.K. (1976). Co-operative Dairying - Our Experience in Jalgaon, Maharashtra. National Co-operative Dairy Federation of India, Bulletin.

Choubey, B.N. (1965). Motivation in co-operatives. *Indian Coop. Rev.*, 2 (4).

Chouhan, J.P.S. (1979). A study of some socio-personal, economic and entrepreneurial characteristics in relation to entrepreneurial role performance of milk products of Karnal city, Unpublished M.Sc. Thesis, Kurukshetra University, Kurukshetra.

Dabas, J.P.S. (1984). An evaluative study of Operation Flood Programme in India. Unpublished M.Sc. Thesis, Kurukshetra University, Kurukshetra.

Dave, D.H. (1975). A study of factors influencing adoption of some important animal husbandry practices in progressive and non-progressive villages of Anand Taluka. Unpublished M.Sc. Thesis, Gujarat Agril. University, Sardar Krishi Nagar, Anand.

Desai, H.N. (1978). A study of leadership characteristics in selected societies of the Kaira District Co-operative Milk Producers' Union Ltd. (AMUL), Anand. Unpublished M.Sc. Thesis, NDRI, Karnal.

Dharamraj, R. (1979). A study of co-operative educational needs and method of education of members and leaders of co-operatives in Pollachi Block. Unpublished M.A. Coop. Thesis, Coimbatore, Sri Rama Krishna Mission Vidyalaya.

Doornbos, M.; Dorston, F.V.; Mitra, M.; and Terhal, P. (1990). *Dairy Aid and Development, India's Operation Flood*. Sage Publications, New Delhi.

Dubey, V.K.; Ram, K.; and Sagar, S.L. (1978) Dynamics of Dairy Cooperatives - Case Studies. *Division of Dairy Extension*, NDRI, Karnal.

Essman, M.J. (1978). Development administration and constituency organisation. *Public Administration Review*, 38: 166-172.

George, S. (1985). *Operation Flood: An Appraisal of Current Indian Dairy Policy*. Oxford Press, Delhi.

George, S. (1985). Operation Flood and Rural India, vested and divested interests. *Economic and Political Weekly*, 20 (7 Dec., 1985) : 2163-2170.

Gopala K., and Maraty, P. (1989). Impact of primary milk producers' co-operative societies on beneficiaries in Nalgonda district of Andhra Pradesh. *Indian Coop. Review*, 26(3) : 278-282.

Gupta, H.C. (1974). How best to provide technical inputs and services needed most by milk producers for optimum results. Dairying as an Instrument of Change, XIX Intern. Dairy Congress, Delhi.

Gurcharan and Degra, B. (1984). Operation flood and dairy development in villages around Delhi. *Economic and Political Weekly*, 19 (20-27 Oct., 1984): 1816-1817.

Guruswami, P.A. and Chinnaiyan, R. (1970). Characteristics of Village co-operative leaders in Tamil Nadu. *Indian Cooperative Review*, 8(1) : 33.

Halse, M. (1980). *Increasing the Incomes of Landless Labourers and Small Holders. Part-I: The Experience of Indian Dairy Cooperatives*. Agricultural Administration and Extension, Anand, Gujarat.

Hashim, S.R. (1989). Rural development - The Indian Experience. *Yojna*, 33 (14-15) : 34-38.

Institute of Rural Management (1981). Tharwata : Report of the Field Visit by the Guntur Team, IRMA, Anand.

Jain, D. (1979). Milk producers of Khaira. In *Women's Quest for Power: Five Indian Cases*, Sahibabad.

Jalal, R.S. (1983). Problems and progress of Dairy co-operatives in Northern hilly region of U.P. *Indian Co-operative Review*, 21(1).

Jha, L.K. (1984). Report of the evaluation committee on Operation Flood-II. Ministry of Agriculture and Fisheries, New Delhi.

Jones, G.N. (1970) Monetary Model of Development : Towards a strategy of large scale planned change, *Philippines J. Pub. Admn.*, 14 (1970): 414 - 435.

Joshi, V.H. (1990). Operation Flood : Constraints and potentialities in Saurashtra. In : Martin Doornbos and K.N. Nair (eds.). *Resources, Institutions and Strategies : Operation Flood and Indian Dairying*, Sage Publications, Delhi.

Kakade, S.D. (1983) Correlates of Executive Members participation in management of primary milk producers co-operative society, Unpublished M.Sc. thesis, submitted to Kurukshetra University, Kurukshetra.

Kanungo, K. (1958). A note on current survey into some aspects of co-operative farming in western U.P. and Punjab. *Indian J. Agril. Econ.*, 13(1) : 90.

Kerlinger, F.N. (1964). *Foundations of Behavioural Research.* Holt Rinehart & Winston Inc., USA:29.

Khandalwala, P.N. (1977). *The Design of Organisations.* ISBN, Delhi.

Khanna, R.S. (1994). Historical developments and evaluation of dairying in India. XXV Dairy Industry Conference, 24-25 March, 1994, New Delhi, pp. 27-45.

Kohli, P.A. (1978). Dairy Co-operatives. *Indian Co-operative Review*, 15 (4).

Kolla, V. (1980). Dynamics of Dairy Cooperatives, case studies in Guntur district (A.P.). Unpublished M.Sc. Thesis, NDRI, Karnal.

Korten, D.C. (1980). Community organisation and rural development - A learning process approach. *Public Administration Review*, 40.

Korten, D.C. (1984). Strategic organisation for people centred development. *Public Administration Review*, 44.

Kretch, D. and Cruchfield, R.S. (1948). *Theory and Problems of Social Psychology*. McGraw Hill Book Co., New York.

Krishnaraj, R. (1981). An analysis of organisational efficiency of milk producers' co-operative society—A systems approach. Unpublished Ph.D. Thesis, Kurukshetra University, Kurukshetra.

Krishnaraj, R. and Dubey, V.K. (1990). Managerial traits associated with organisational efficiency of milk producers' co-operative society. *Indian J. Dairy Science*, 41 (1) : 19-23.

Kulandaisamy, V. (1984). Dairy Co-operatives and rural development. The Indian Experience. *Review of International Co-operation*, 77(1) : 38-41.

Kulkarni, K.R. (1959). *Theory and Practices of Co-operation in India and Abroad.* Vol.2, Second Ed., Co-operator Book Depot, Bombay.

Kurien, V. (1984). *Interview with Manoshi Mitra*, Anand, Feb. 3.

Laidlaw, Alex (1975). I have seen it. The Maritime Co-operator. Cited from reprint reproduced by Amul, Anand.

Lerman, Z. and Parliament, C. (1989). *Industry and Size Effects in*

Agricultural Co-operatives, Staff Paper, Department of Agricutural and Applied Economics, University of Minnesota, pp. 89-140:18 pp, USA.

Mahipal (1975). A study of the role performance of multipurpose co-operative society leaders in relation to their socio-psychological characteristics. Unpublished M.Sc. Thesis, IARI, New Delhi.

Mahipal and Rai, G.C. (1978). Role performance of the leaders of efficient and non-efficient multipurpose co-operative societies. *Indian J. of Exten. Edu.*, 14 (1 & 2).

Menon, M.N. (1977) Made for each other, paper presented at 13th Dairy Industry Conference held at Hissar (Haryana), April, 6-8, 1977, Dairying in India - 77.

Mescarenhas, R.C. (1988). *A Strategy for Rural Development: Dairy Co-operative in India*. Sage Publications, New Delhi.

Meti, T.K. (1965).Co-operatives in development perspective. *Indian Co-operative Review*, 2(4).

Mishra, N.P. and Ram, B. (1966). The role of service co-operative in agricultural production *Ind. J. of Extn. Edu.*, Vol. 2 (1 & 2).

Mishra, A.A.; Awasthi, P.K.; and Jaiswal, D.K. (1987). Constraints in utilization of farm technology in Madhya Pradesh. Paper presented in the Seminar on Constraints in TOT, held at KKV, Dapoli, Oct. 20-30.

Mitra, M. (1990). Anand in Bihar : Replication of Caste and Class Patterns. Quoted from *Resources, Institutions and Strategies*. Edited by Doornbos *et al.*, Sage Publications, New Delhi.

Nataraju, M.S. and Channegowda, M.B. (1987). A study of knowledge and adoption behaviour of cattle owners. *Mysore J. Agric. Sci.*, 21(3) : 354-358.

Nath, V. (1973). Factors responsible for success or failure of co-operative sugarcane supply society—A micro approach. *Indian Co-operative Review*, 10(4):455.

N.C.A. (1976). Abridged Report, Govt. of India, Ministry of Agriculture and Irrigation, New Delhi, p. 306.

Oren, A. and Herman, Z. (1986). A Survey of the Farm Management Co-operative Association : Proposals for the development and irrigation of four dairy farms. Division for International Co-operation, Jerusalem, Israel.

Panda, R.C. (1979). Role of women in Dairy Co-operatives: Manjini Cooperative Milk Supply Society. Paper presented at a Workshop on Women's Participation in Dairy Co-operatives in India, NDDB, Anand.

Pandey, M.K. (1981). *Economics of Milk Production in Rural Areas of Baroda District*. Institute of Coop. Management, Baroda.

Patel, B.T. (1980). A study of factors influencing successful functioning of village milk producers' co-operative societies in Kaira district of Gujarat. Unpublished Ph.D. Thesis, IARI, New Delhi.

Patel, R.K. and Das, C.S. (1979). Dairying through small and marginal farmers and the landless. *Indian Dairyman*, 31(3) : 177.

Patel, S.M.; Thakur, D.S.; and Pandey, M.K. (1975). *Impact of the Milk Co-operatives in Gujarat*. United Publishers, Katra Road, Allahabad.

Patel, T.D. (1973). Organizational structure for increased milk production. Xth Dairy Industry Conference, Madras, *Indian Dairyman*, 25(5) : 192.

Patel, Y.A. and Mradulla, V.K. (1974). Adoption of improved practices in village Bajipura. *Kurukshetra*, Sept. 17.

Patil, S.O. and Sawant, G.K. (1978). Characteristics of members of co-operative society. *Indian Coop. Review*, 10(3) : 303-310.

P.E.O. (1960). *Evaluation Report of Operation Flood*. Planning Commission, Govt. of India., New Delhi.

Porter, L.W.; Stress, R.H.; Day, R.T.; and Boulian, P.U. (1974). Organisational commitment questionnaire. Cited from Halold, L. Angle and James, L.R. (1981). An empirical assessment of organisational commitment and organisational effectiveness. *Administrative Science Quarterly*, 26(1) : 1-13.

Puri, S.S. (1973). Co-operative an assessment of work and growth. *Indian Co-operative Review*, 10 (3): 303.

Raju, D.T. and Maraty, P. (1991). How to popularise crossbred cows? *Yojna*, 35(5) : 25.

Ram, C.V. and Kalla, J.C. (1983). Appraisal of investment viability of a dairy development co-operative federation in North-West India. *Indian J. Agric. Econ.*, 38(1) :

Rath, B.B. (1977). A critical analysis of an ICDP : Progress, Problems and Prospects. Unpublished Ph.D. Thesis, H.A.U., Hisar.

Saini, S.P.S. (1975). A study of factors affecting adoption of selected recommended dairy practices. Unpublished M.Sc. Thesis, P.A.U., Ludhiana.

Selznick, P. (1966). *Leadership in Administration*. New York, Harper & Row, pp. 5-22.

Shah, T. (1987). Structural effects of India's dairy co-operatives and the technological transformation of a traditional dairy system. *Agricultural Administration and Extension*, 24(4), Anand, Gujarat.

Sheoran, V.K. (1987). A study of adoption level of dairy innovations in relation to milk yield among beneficiaries of IRDP in district Karnal, Haryana. Unpublished M.Sc. Thesis, Kurukshetra University, Kurukshetra.

Shroti, A.K. (1989). An analysis of constraints in milk procurement in milk producers' co-operative union limited, Aligarh. Unpublished M.Sc. Thesis, NDRI, Karnal.

Sidhu, J.S. and Sidhu, R.S. (1990). Case studies of successful and unsuccessful primary co-operative service society and milk producers' co-operative societies in India. *Indian J. Agric. Econ.*, 45(3) : 367-378.

Singh, A.K. (1995). *Performance of Milk Co-operatives in Haryana and Gujarat - A Comparative Study,* Ph.D. Thesis, N.D.R.I. Karnal.

Singh, J. (1990) Reduction of losses in operation of milk co-operatives. *Indian Dairyman*, 42(3) : 131-134.

Singh, K. (1987). *Managing Dairy Development Experiences and Lessons from Amul. Some Issues in Development Administration*, Oxford & IBH Publishing Co., New Delhi, pp.142-166.

Singh, K. and Das, M. (1984). Impact of Operation Flood at Village Level. *Indian J. Agric. Econ.*, 39(2) : 212-214.

Singh, R. (1992). A study of constraints in the functioning of milk producers' co-operative societies in Western U.P. Unpublished Ph.D. Thesis, NDRI, Karnal.

Singh, S. (1987). Functional efficiency of milk producers' co-operative societies in Bhiwani district of Haryana (Case Studies). Unpublished M.Sc. Thesis, Kurukshetra University, Kurukshetra.

Singh, S. (1989). A study of differential level of knowledge and adoption of dairy innovations by farmers in the adopted villages of Dairy Extension Division, NDRI, Karnal. Unpublished M.Sc. Thesis, NDRI, Karnal.

Singh, S. (1994). An analysis of adopters' categories of dairy innovations in relation to their socio-economic and psychological characteristics. Unpublished Ph.D. Thesis, NDRI, Karnal.

Singh, S.P. and Kelly, P.L. (1981). *Amul—An Experiment in Rural Economic Development*. Macmillan, New Delhi.

Singh, V. (1984). *Impact of Mini Dairy Scheme of District Karnal* (Haryana). unpublished M.Sc. Thesis, Kurukshetra University, Kurukshetra.

Sohal, T.S. (1973). Barriers in popularising Dairy Farming. *Haryana Review*, 7(7) : 45.

Somzee, G. and Somzee, A.H. (1989). *Reaching Out To The Poor : The Unfinished Rural Revolution*. MacMillan Press, U.K.

Srivastava, R.M., (1969). Factors affecting functioning of village milk producers' co-operative societies of Kaira district, Gujarat State. Unpublished M.Sc. Thesis, Vallabh Vidyanagar, Sardar Patel University.

Srivastava, R.M. (1982). Cattle culture and economy of tribal Mundas of Bihar. Unpublished Ph.D. Thesis, Kurukshetra University, Kurukshetra.

Subramanian, R. (1982) Study of Technological and socio-economic impact of milk co-operatives in Erode district (Tamil Nadu), Unpublished Ph.D. thesis, Kurukshetra University, Kurukshetra.

Supe, S.P. (1966). The study of opinion and attitude of cultivators towards co-operatives. *Magazine of College of Agriculture*, Akola, 6(1).

Supe, S.V. and Kulkarni, B.B. (1972). Psychological characteristics of service co-operative members. *Society and Culture*, 3(2).

Supe, S.V. and Singh, S.N. (1969). *Dynamics of Rational Behaviour of Indian Farmers*. New Heights Publishers and Distributors, Delhi.

Swami, T.K. (1980). Dynamics of Dairy Co-operatives - Case studies in Karnataka. Unpublished M.Sc. Thesis, Kurukshetra University, Kurukshetra.

Twade, N.D.; Patil, S.D.; and Wadkar, S.S. (1987). Analysis of communication barriers in extension work of agricultural extension officers. Paper presented in the Seminar on TOT held at KKV, Dapoli, Oct. 20-30.

Ulrey, O. (1966). The co-operative. An agency for Rural Development (The Kaira District Cooperative Ltd., Anand, Gujarat State, India). Agricultural Economics Report No. 42, East Honsing, Michigan State University.

UN/FAO (1981). *World Food Programme*. Terminal Project Report, pp.61-63.

Venkatasubramanian, V. and Fulzele, R.M. (1996). *Dairy Farming in Tropics*, MD Publishers, 11, Daryaganj, New Delhi.

Verhagen, M. (1990). Operation Flood and the Rural Poor. In : M. Doornbos and K.N. Nair (eds.). *Resources Institutions and Strategies: Operation Flood and Indian Dairying*, Sage Publications, New Delhi.

Verma, O.P. (1988). A study on impact of technical inputs and services on the milk production enhancement in Barabanki District Co-operative Milk Union Ltd. Unpublished M.Sc. Thesis, NDRI, Karnal.

Verma, O.P. (1993). A study of impact of milk co-operative societies in Upper Gangetic Plains. Unpublished Ph.D. Thesis, NDRI, Karnal.

Vithol, C.P. (1986). Factors affecting milk co-operatives in Anantapur District of Andhra Pradesh - A case study. *Indian Coop. Review*, 23 (4).

Walia, A.P.S. (1984). Impact of technical input services on the milk production enhancement in milkshed area of Ludhiana Milk Plant (Punjab). Unpublished M.Sc. Thesis, Kurukshetra University, Kurukshetra.

Yadav, S.S. (1986). A study of training needs of rural youth in Haryana. Unpublished M.Sc. Thesis, Kurukshetra University, Kurukshetra.

6

ECONOMICS OF DAIRY EXTENSION AND DEVELOPMENT

Introduction

India was the first country to adopt a community development programme which emphasized improvement in agricultural practices, health care and education. Introduced social change through its development programmes and encouraged self-help to create within the local people the feeling of participation in development. The scheme of community development which was first introduced in 55 extension blocks in 1952 was subsequently extended to cover the entire country. The programme was developed on the basis of the encouraging result of the pilot project which introduced community development in sixty-four villages in Etawah district of U.P. in 1948. The success of Etawah was seen as blue print for extending it to the rest of the country. However, its extension did not take into account the political, economical and bureaucratic impediments which were not encountered at Etawah. For a country of India's size and dimensions any effort of replicating Etawah based on the results of the pilot project would prove very expensive in terms of resources. Alternatively, it became a conflict of equity *versus* quality and under the compulsions of democratic participation of rural people, widespread extension rendered cheaper by diluting or overlooking some underlying lessons of the pilot project was preferred. Thus, community development programmes were extended to the entire country for reasons of equity and as a device for political mobilisation to fill the rural vacuum (Mascarenhas, 1988). Similarly, other extension programmes such as IADP, ICDP, milk co-operative societies were also extended indiscriminately on the basis of their initial success in few areas. Our question here is what were the consequences of these programmes. For an extension programme the project choice is somewhat more complex. In choosing projects the planner has to ascertain the ones that best satisfy the interests and objectives of the nation.

What are the economic and social costs and benefits of the projects chosen for implementation? When an extension project is implemented the consequences in terms of output, employment, consumption, savings, income distribution and other intangible benefits are to be thought of (Orievel, 1983). The purpose of economics of extension is to see whether these consequences taken together are desirable in the light of the farmers and objectives of national planning. Therefore, the consequences brought by an extension project must be evaluated from all the dimensions including economics which is essential for making a sound extension policy.

Studies in the Evaluation of Extension

The literature on the evaluation of extension has been summarized by Orievel (1983). The evaluation of extension has been attempted from a variety of perspectives with mixed results. Some, usually aggregative studies (e.g., Evenson and Jha, 1973) recognizing the dependence of extension on agricultural research, combine the two and have shown a positive relationship between them and agricultural productivity. Harker (1973) attempted to find out the effects of extension by comparing the farmers who have contact with extension agents with those who do not. These evaluations under-estimate the effects by not taking into account the way in which information once acquired by one farmer can be passed on to the others. The impact of the dairy co-operative on the adoption of innovations by the farmers have been studied by a number of researchers (Rao, 1975; Mikkilienin, 1976; Nachiappan and Srinivasamurthy, 1976; Puthusamy, 1976; Sidhu, 1980; Patel, 1980; and Subramanian, 1982). Other studies have concentrated in assessing extension performance by measuring the extent of farmer-extension agent interactions (e.g. Chambers and Wickeremanayake, 1977). Few studies have examined the extent to which the visits of extension agents are biased in favour of rich and influential farmers (Leonard, 1973). Lockheed *et al.* (1980) studied the relationship between education and farmer productivity as an effect of extension. Such studies shed little light on the net benefits of extension. For that a rigorous comparative analysis to observe whether the effects commensurate with the costs incurred to produce them should be attempted. The studies conducted in developed countries are much more rigorous than those conducted in developing countries. Benor and Harrison (1977) evaluated the T&V system in India by simply comparing the before and after crop yield. Such studies, however, do not indentify and hence evaluate the contribution of extension in increasing the output because they do not separate out the contributions of factors such as material inputs, soil quality, supply constraints and other variables likely to influence the output (Feder and Slade, 1985). The rapid spread of the T&V system has given rise to claims of tangible success (Benor and Harrison, 1977) and also provoked considerable criticism. But both proponents and critics lack substantive and objective empirical evidences to substantiate their claims.

Need for Economic Evaluation of Extension

At present, the Indian Extension system deals with 81.5 million land holdings and about 500 million farmers, including farm women, young farmers and agricultural labourers (Prasad *et al.*, 1987). Extension programmes are an investment activity where we expend capital resources to create functional units at grassroots level from which we can expect to realise the benefits over an extended period of time. Evaluation is the process of determining how well one is doing in what one is trying to do (USDA, 1956). Evaluation when applied to the field of extension, may be defined as "a process of systematic appraisal by which we determine the value, worth or consequences of an extension programme/activity. Twenty years of T&V experience has taught us that there can be no one system of extension suited to all farming communities. Extension is at the interface between demand and supply systems of agricultural technology (Hayward, 1989). Most of the studies conducted in India to assess the T & V system were of mostly comparison of yield rates before and after the implementation of the programme. However, it must be understood that evaluation is not simply a measurement of achievements, which is usually done after a programme is executed. A complete evaluation for extension is one which aims at the full length enumeration of both tangible and intangible costs and benefits involved. Both tangible costs and benefits are easy to identify but it is not so for intangible ones. Knowledge, once disseminated by the extension service and acquired by farmers, has a tangible measurable product only if applied (Orievel, 1983; Feder and Slade, 1985). The application of such knowledge by farmers is generally termed as adoption and is usually measured by adoption rates, that is, the proportion of farmers applying knowledge of a particular technology that they have acquired from extension agents. Moreover, adoption cannot take place without knowledge. It is not an automatic consequence of the acquisition of knowledge as many other influences may affect a farmer's decision to adopt. Among these are the profitability of the technology, the availability of key inputs, credit and complementary knowledge (Fitzhugh *et al.*, 1982). Moreover, many of the services of the animal production technology are often not available to the resource-poor farmers living in remote areas, and clients of these services are usually semi-commercial farmers who benefit from such technology (Pervaiz and Hendrik, 1989). So it is not entirely correct and complete method of evaluating the extension through the adoption rate alone. An application of the economic concept in the evaluation of extension projects brings about the tota' net cost and benefit of the project.

Various Stages/Phases in Economic Evaluation of Extension

Where does economic evaluation fit into extension programmes? Economic evaluation is a part and parcel of all phases in an extension programme right from its initial planning to implementation and completion. The economic concept of extension is applied:

(1) at project selection,
(2) during implementation, and
(3) after completion of the project.

Evaluation Criteria during Project Selection

An extension project can be either selected or rejected once its cost and benefits are identified and valued. Moreover, the realistic estimation of costs and benefits is a pre-requisite for the successful evaluation of an extension project at its selection stage. Most of the extension projects suffer from incomplete identification usually resulting into over-estimation of benefits and under-estimation of costs (Evenson, 1978). The compounding and discounting are the techniques to enable the benefits and costs streams (or cash inflow and cash outflow) from different projects at a particular point of time to examine the profitability of each project and relative profitability of the projects.

Usually, a wide range of criteria are applied to evaluate a project during the selection stage for choosing the investment proposals. These criteria are classified into (1) Non-discounting criteria which includes urgency, payback period and accounting rate of return for estimation, and (2) Discounting criteria which includes the Net present worth, Internal rate of return, Benefit-cost ratio and Net Benefit Investment Ratio as its tool. The figures obtained during the initial stage of project selection are purely on the basis of conceptual ideas. This has to be confirmed before actually implementing the project on a large scale. This could be done through conducting on field extension trials and evaluating the results.

Economic Analysis of On Field Extension Trials (OFET)

The consequences expected out of selected extension projects and technologies that are to be transferred to the farmers can be assessed by carrying out the evaluation of On Field Extension Trials (OFET) under different client group settings. The objective here is to ascertain the initial estimated cost and benefits of the project on its large scale implementation. This OFET will help us as a screening tool in eliminating the extension projects and technologies which are not viable before going for a large scale implementation. The initial cost-benefit estimates worked out at the time of project selection is purely based on the projected and conceptual figures whereas results of the OFET gives us the estimates nearer to the real costs and benefits of the project on its large scale implementation.

Although the need to develop bio-economic models to screen new technologies has been stressed (Fitzhugh, 1978), data are so limited that such complex models can be developed only in advanced countries. They become mere academic exercises when applied to developing country situation (Pervaiz and Hendrik, 1989). Even though the OFET can guide research, evaluation as well as to identify the weaknesses in the extension system, such models rarely conceived and tried in the practical situation because the models suffer with various limitations. Demonstration farm models have widely been used to conduct the economic analysis of OFET.

The demonstration farm approach has helped to determine

the economic value of new dairy technology for different sizes of farms (Patel, 1981). The yield-gap model gives the difference between the yields that are technical and economically feasible and the actual yields obtained by majority of the farmers. This model presented by Gomez and Santos (1981) is mainly used to explain the differences in the performance of technology at the farmers farm and research station (Fig. 6.1). What is the effect of extension in reducing this gap? Only an effective evaluation will give the answer.

Production differences

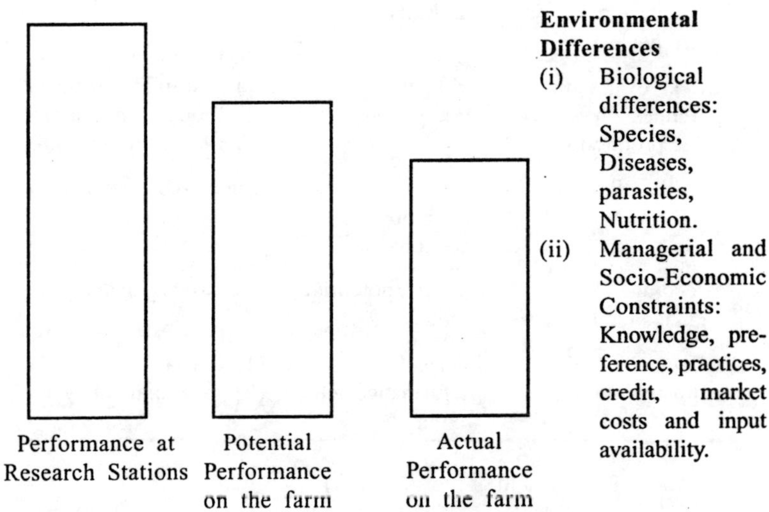

Fig. 6.1 : Yield Gap Model

The profitability of an extension programme should be verified through giving special attention to the identification of net costs and benefits of the technology to be transferred. In the preliminary stage, profitability should be estimated at the optimal input levels, with appropriate discount for risk. In addition farmers should be consulted to identify the inputs, such as cash, labour, training requirements that play a part in the decision to experiment with the new technology which is to be implemented through the existing extension system. An evaluation that takes into account only the cash inputs (such as gross margin analysis) may be appropriate for certain type of technologies only (Pervaiz and Hendrik, 1989). Table 6.1 shows how economic tools can be matched for screening the technologies involved in animal production before incorporating into the extension system.

Table 6.1 : Economic tools for screening the technologies

Technology	Farmers criteria	Tools of analysis
Effects of new yoke design on draft power	Weight and durability	Benefit-cost analysis
Effect of feeding practices on milk production	Changes in milk yield	(1) Marginal analysis (2) Production function (3) Linear programming
Health related	Disease prevention and control	Benefit-cost analysis
Breeding and Management	Genetic potential production	Gross-margin analysis
Effects of feed supplementation	Physical performance and weight gain	(1) Partial budgeting (2) Financial analysis

Source : Pervaiz and Hendrik (1989).

Cost-Benefit Analysis in Extension

"Every possible thing in this world is at some cost". The net cost and benefit in any extension programme includes both tangible and intangible costs. According to this, we cannot ignore the social cost (which is intangible) which the society incur on the execution of the programme. Even though it is intangible, it is considered for the cost estimation because of the social value attached to it. The difficulties involved in measuring the social cost benefit is anybody's imagination. Yet without the inclusion of these intangible costs the efforts to evaluate the extension largely remains non-functional.

The social cost is anything the society pays/sacrifices save monetary contributions for the execution of an extension programme. Likewise the social benefits are those benefits other than its monetary benefits derived from the outcome of the project on its execution. Mostly, the social cost and benefits are indirect in nature.

Vaccination compaigns and knowledge about the animal diseases directly reduced the number of animals affected by the diseases and indirectly improved the relationship between the village rival groups as no longer the farmers believe the ailment of his animals as the handiwork of his village witchcraft and rival group. The extension programme brings knowledge to the farmers and their family. In a broader sense, the cost of bringing out the knowledge to the family can be worked out but what the knowledge brings/does to the farm family is multi-dimensional in nature in which the economic benefit is one of its dimensions. The other dimensions are, due to increase in production, the farmer becomes economically well-off and his sons and daughters could get educated and take up new occupations. What about the services rendered by these newly benefited classes to their society? Is it an outcome of extension or not? How we can cover all these dimensions while attempting to measure the social cost and benefit of the extension? Is it possible to cover all its dimensions or not? If yes, up to what extent, if not what are the impeding forces and alternatives perceived? These are the questions, which need to be answered. Still there is no definite criteria or standardized procedures or ways to measure the social cost and benefit in the extension. As already stated, the economic cost-benefit is one aspect of the whole which we have to measure for determining a project's worth. It is the responsibility of the social scientists to take up this issue for attempting a complete evaluation of extension in this direction.

The final step in the evaluation required that the value of the increase in farm output resulting from our estimates of the productivity differential attributable to extension, be set against the additional costs incurred to make the additional output possible. To do so, the familiar technique of cost-benefit analysis has to be applied to the extension system. As the analysis has to be undertaken ex-post availability of a complete series of either costs or benefits for the entire life of the project will help in arriving at an accurate evaluation result. If the costs and benefits for the entire life of the project is not available, we have to make a number of assumptions relevant of an ex-ante analysis (Feder and Slade, 1985).

The stream of incremental extension costs should be constructed using data on the actual costs of the project during the initial years. In scenarios where the project life was assured to be less than the life span of physical structures and equipments, appropriate residual values were calculated and deducted from the costs (Feder and Slade, 1985). For arriving at an actual impact of extension, the econometric techniques which accounted for differences in the quantities of variables and fixed inputs, the type of soils, human capital, and the production environment are used to estimate the percentage output differentials between the two areas with and without extension. Such an approach implies that when differences in variable inputs are controlled, the effect (if any) of extension on input use is ignored between the operational and non-operational areas. If differences in the use of variable inputs are not taken into account then the output differential includes the effect of extension on farm efficiency as well as the effect on the use of inputs, provided that price differentials are also controlled (Feder and Slade, 1985). A complete accounting for the effects of extension should, therefore, take both types of effect into account. A simplified graphical representation of these effects were given by the Feder and Slade (Fig. 6.2) while explaining the

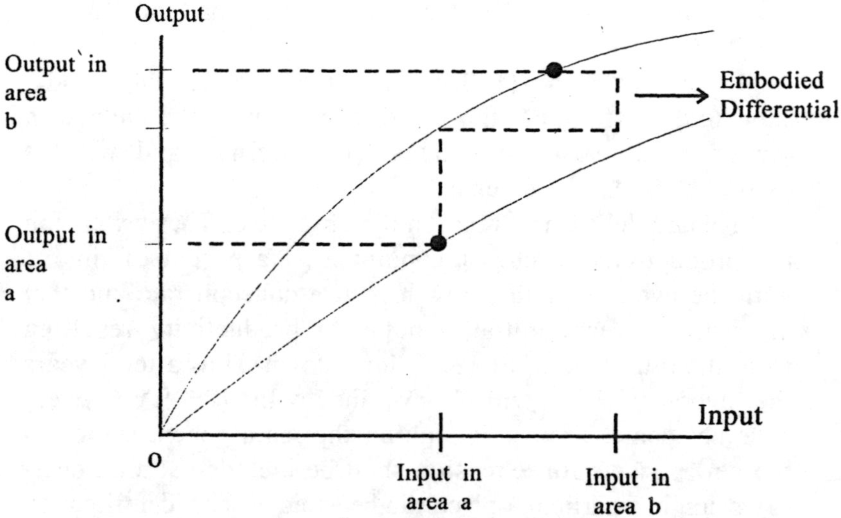

Fig. 6.2 : Embodied and disembodied productivity differential (Feder and Slade, 1985)

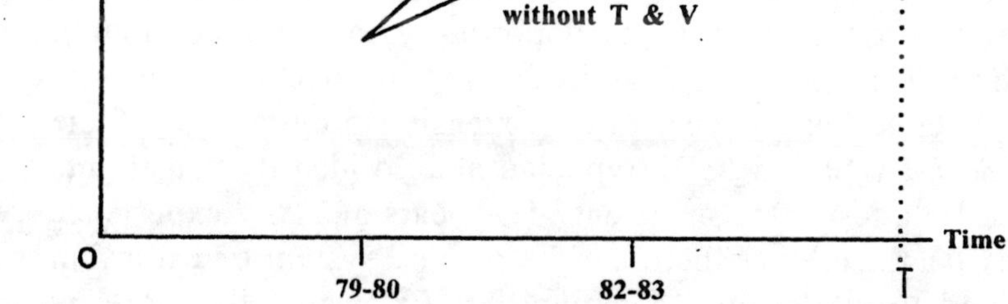

Fig 6.3: Time pattern of Productivity Change is the productivity gain due to extension in 1982-83 (Feder and Slade, 1985).

impact of T & V system of extension in Karnal and Kairana tehsil in 1979.

Feder and Slade (1985) constructed yet another model (Fig. 6.3) to stimulate the future evolution of the change in the productivity in both areas with (Karnal) and without (Kairana) T & V extension.

This model assumes that in the absence of T&V extension the productivity reaches the point *X* at a period of time *T* with the average yield growth is at a constant rate and that after a few years initial impetus to productivity resulting from the introduction of T&V slows down. Thus after *T* years the average yield with T&V and without T&V system becomes same. From this finding the main generalisation is the new pockets for extension shall be included so that over-extension in a particular place can be avoided. The identification of the point where the extension support shall be withdrawn is more crucial for the extension so that the efforts can be concentrated in areas where the output for given unit of extension is more.

Summary

On the basis of the above discussions, it is concluded that extension projects are the cutting edge of dairy development. The project is a whole complex of activities undertaken to achieve an objective. Extension education programmes will not be very effective in influencing rapid dairy development, unless producers have the opportunity to use a continuing flow of animal productivity increasing technologies at acceptable benefit cost ratio. Extension programmes of the T & V, IADP and ICDP type can help to identify constraints and field test solution. Twenty-five years of T & V experience has taught us that there can be no one system of extension suited to all farming communities. Extension, therefore, is at the interface between demand and supply systems of agricultural technology. This is very much true with respect to dairy development programmes also.

For a complete evaluation of an extension programme, all the dimensions of the programmes should be taken into consideration. CBA is a practical way of appraising the desirability of a project involving public expenditure in terms of net social gains to the society. In many of the impact studies conducted in our extension research this particular aspect of the evaluation is missing and so it is advocated for attempting the evaluation of extension in this dimension also which certainly throws more light on the project's worth.

References

Benor, D. and Harrison, J.Q. (1977). *Agricultural Extension. The Training and Visit System*. The World Bank. Washington D.C.

Brown, D.D. (1971). *Agricultural Development in Indian Districts*. Hardward University Press, Cambridge.

Chambers, R. and Vickre Manayake, (1977). Agricultural Extension: Myth, Reality and Challenge. *In Farmer (and) Green Revolution*, Westview Press, Boulder, Colorado.

Chawla, K.L. (1980). *Social Cost Benefit Analysis*. Planning, Implementation and Evaluation of Agricultural Projects. (Ed.) Indian Institute of Public Administration, New Delhi.

Evenson, R.E. (1978). Research, Invention, Extension and Productivity Change in US Agriculture: A Historical Decomposition Analysis. Paper Presented at Symposium on Research and Extension Evaluation. Moscow, Idaho, 21-23 May.

Evenson, R.E. and Jha, D. (1973). The Contribution of Agricultural Research System to Agricultural Production System in India. *Indian Journal of Agricultural Economics,* Vol. B, pp. 212-230.

Feder, G. and Slade, R. (1984). A Comparative Analysis of Some Aspects of the Training and Visit System of Agricultural Extension in India (Washington DC: Research Unit, Agricultural and Rural Development Department, World Bank).

Fitzhugh, H.A. (1976). "Bio-Economic Analysis of Ruminant Production System". *J. Animal Science*, 43(3).

Fitzhugh, H.A.; Hart, R.D.; Moreno, R.A.; Dsuja, D.D.; Ruiz, M.E.; and Singh, L. (1982). :Research on Crop Animal Systems, Central Agronomic Tropical de Investigation Y Ensenomaya/Carobbean Agricultural Development Institute/Winrock-International, Morrilton, AR, USA.

Gomez and Santos (1981). *Conducting on Farm-Animal Research: Procedures and Economic Analysis* by Pervaiz, A. and Hendrik, C.K. 1989. (Cited from) Winrock International Institute for Agricultural Development and IDRC, USA & Canada.

Harker, B.R. (1973). The Contribution of Schooling to Agricultural Modernization: An Empirical Analysis in P. Foster and R.J. Sheffield (eds). *Education and Rural Development*. London : Evans Brothers.

Hayward, J.A. (1989). "Failure Directions in Agricultural Extension". World Bank, Paper presented at the ISREP, Wageningen. Published by International Agricultural Centre, Wageningen, The Netherlands.

Khurody, D.N. (1974). *Dairying in India - A Review*. Asia Publishing House, Bombay p. 105.

Leonard, D. (1973). Why do Kenya's Agricultural Extension Services Favour the Rich Farmer? Sixteenth Annual Meeting of the African Studies Association, Syracuse, N.Y.

Lockheed, M.E., Jamison, D.T. and Lau, L.J. (1980). Farmer Education and Farm efficiency : A survey. *Economic Development and Cultural Change*. Vol. 29, No.1, Oct.

Mascarenhas, R.C. (1988). *A Strategy for Rural Development: Dairy Co-operatives in India*. Sage Publications, New Delhi.

Mikkilinenin, V.K. (1976). *A Study of Adaption of A Few Selected Dairy Practices in Upland and Delta Areas of Vijayawada Taluk*, Krishna district (A.P.) M.Sc. Thesis, Kurukshetra University, Kurukshetra.

Nachiappan and Srinivasamurthy (1976). "The impact of SFDA on the knowledge of participant small farmers of Tamil Nadu". *Indian J. Extn. Edu.*, 13(384): 65-66.

Orievel, Froncois, (1983). "Basic Education and Agricultural Extension—Costs, Effects and Alternatives." World Bank Staff Working Papers Number 564. Washington D.C., USA. P. 4-53.

Patel, B.T. (1980). *A Study of Factors Influencing Successful Functioning of Village Milk Producers Co-op. Societies in Kaira District of Gujarat*, Ph.D. Thesis, IARI, New Delhi.

Patel, R.K. (1981). "Economics of livestock enterprises with special reference to its employment potential". *Indian J. Agricultural Economics*, 36(1).

Pervaiz, Amir and Hendrik, C.K. (1989). *Conducting On-Farm Animal Research: Procedures of Economic Analysis*, Winrock International Institute for Agricultural Development and International Development Research Centre, USA & Canada.

Prasad, C.; Chowdhary, B.N.; and Bhatnagar, B. (1987). First line of Transfer of Technological Projects. Publication and Information Division. ICAR, New Delhi.

Puthusamy, T. (1976). *A Study on Knowledge Adoption and Attitude of Small Farmers towards Mixed Farming in Sirsa and Arekal Taluka*, Thesis Abstract, HAU,, Hisar.

Raman, K.V.; Balaguru, T.; and Manikandan, P. (1988). *National Agricultural Research, Education and Extension Education System in India.* National Academy of Agricultural Research Management, Hyderabad.

Rao, B.S. (1975). *A Study of the Combined Impact of Dairy Co-operatives and ICDP on Socio-economic Changes in the Milkshed Areas of Bhongir* (A.P.). M.Sc. Thesis, NDRI, Karnal. Kurukshetra University, Kurukshetra.

Saroja, S. (1988). *Planning, Implementation and Evaluation of Agricultural Projects* (Ed.) Indian Institute of Public Administration, New Delhi.

Sidhu, K.S. (1980). "A study of the dimensional variation in the knowledge of dairy farmers of ICDP and non-ICDP areas of Punjab," M.Sc. Thesis, Kurukshetra University, Kurukshetra.

Subramanian, C. (1979). *The New Strategy in Indian Agriculture - The First Decade and After*. Vikas Publishing House, New Delhi pp. 85-86.

Subramanian, R. (1982). *A Study of Technological and Socio-economic Impact of Milk Co-operatives in Erode District (Tamil Nadu).* Ph.D. Thesis, Kurukshetra Univ. Kurukshetra.

USDA, (1957). *Essentials of Sound Extension Programme Development,* Washington D.C. ER & T.

Venkatasubramanian, V. and Fulzele, R.M. (1996). *Dairy Farming in Tropics*, MD Publishers, New Delhi.

Bibliography

Acharya, R.M. (1984) Constraints in Milk Production Enhancement in India, Diamond Jubilee Souvenir (1983-84), NDRI, Karnal.

Baviskar, B.S. (1980). *The Politics of Development : Sugar Co-operatives in Rural Maharashtra*. Oxford University Press, Delhi.

Baviskar, B.S. (1986). Dairy Development in a Tribal Area of Gujarat. Working Papers, Dairy Aid and Development, Institute of Social Studies, The Hague.

Baviskar, B.S. (1990). Dairy cooperatives and rural development in Gujarat. In : M. Doornbos and K.N. Nair (Eds.). *Resources, Institutions and Strategies : Operation Flood and Indian Dairying*, New Delhi, Sage Publications.

Baviskar, B.S. and Terhal, P. (1990). Internal constraints and external dependence : EEC and Operation Flood. In : M. Doornbos and K.N. Nair (eds.). *Resources, Institutions and Strategies : Operation Flood and Indian Dairying*, New Delhi, Sage Publications.

Benor, D. and Harrison, J.Q. (1977). *Agricultural Extension. The Training and Visit System*. The World Bank. Washington, D.C.

Bhatnagar, O.P. (1974). Constraints to the differential acceptance of the components of new agricultural technology. In : Singh, D. and Pandey, J.S. (eds.). *Transfer of Technology System and Constraints*. Pub. "Nirbal-Ke-Balram", Kanpur.

Brown, D.D. (1971). *Agricultural Development in Indian Districts*. Hardward University Press, Cambridge.

Chambers, R. and Vickre Manayake, (1977). Agricultural Extension: Myth, Reality and Challenge. In *Farmer (and) Green Revolution*, Westtrew Press, Boulder, Colorado.

Chawla, K.L. (1980). "Social Cost Benefit Analysis". *Planning, Implementation and Evaluation of Agricultural Projects*. Ed. Indian Institute of Public Administration, New Delhi.

Cook, K.J. (1994). *AMA Complete Guide to Strategic Planning for Small Business*, NTC Publishers Group: Lincoln Wood, Illinois, U.S.A.

Das, A.C Structure of Milk Production in Tamil Nadu: An Analysis of Trends and Sources of Growth. In Doornbos Martin and K. N. Nair (1991), *Resources, Institutions and Strategies: Operation Flood and Indian Dairying*, Sage Publications, New Delhi.

Doornbos, M.; Dorston, F.V.; Mitra, M.; and Terhal, P. (1990). *Dairy Aid and development, India's Operation Flood.* Sage Publications, New Delhi.

George, P.S. and Nair, K.N. (1990). *Livestock Economy of Kerala*, Centre for Development Studies, Trivandrum.

George, S. (1985). *Operation Flood: An Appraisal of Current Indian Dairy Policy.* Oxford Press, Delhi.

Gomez and Santos (1981). "Conducting on Farm-Animal Research: Procedures and Economic Analysis" by Pervaiz, A. and Hendrik, C.K. 1989. (Cited from) Winrock International Institute for Agricultural Development and IDRC, USA & Canada.

Gupta, H.C. (1974). How best to provide technical inputs and services needed most by milk producers for optimum results. Dairying as an Instrument of Change, XIX Intern. Dairy Congress, Delhi.

Hermittte M.A (1989). In Gerald Werner (ed), Animal Genetic Resources - A Global Programme for Sustainable Development, Proceedings of an FAO expert consultation, Rome, pp 13-26.

Institute of Rural Management (1981). Tharwata : Report of the Field Visit by the Guntur Team, IRMA, Anand.

Jose, T.K. (1988). Dairying in Kerala, 22nd Dairy Industry Conference, Trivandrum, 29

Joshi, V.H. (1990). Operation Flood : Constraints and Potentialities in Saurashtra. In : Martin Doornbos and K.N. Nair (eds.). *Resources, Institutions and Strategies : Operation Flood and Indian Dairying*, Sage Publications, Delhi.

Kerlinger, F.N. (1964). *Foundations of Behavioural Research.* Holt Rinehart & Winston Inc., USA:29.

Khurody, D.N. (1974). *"Dairying in India" - A Review.* Asia Publishing House, Bombay p. 105.

Kretch, D. and Cruchfield, R.S. (1948). *Theory and Problems of Social Psychology.* McGraw Hill Book Co., New York.

Leonard, D.G.; Timothy, M.N.; and William, J.P. (1993). *Applied Strategic Planning: A Comprehensive Guide*, McGraw a Hill, Inc.

Mascarenhas, R.C. (1988). *A Strategy for Rural Development: Dairy Co-operatives in India*. Sage Publications, New Delhi.

Mitra, M. (1990). Anand in Bihar : Replication of Caste and Class Patterns. Quoted from *Resources. Institutions and Strategies*. Edited by Doornbos *et al*., Sage Publications, New Delhi.

Mosher, A.T. (1966) Conditions to be met to Accelerate Agricultural Development, Agricultural Development Council, New York.

National Commission on Agriculture (1976). Animal Husbandry Part VII, Ministry of Food and Agriculture, Government of India, New Delhi.

Pandey, M.K. (1981). *Economics of Milk Production in Rural Areas of Baroda district*. Institute of Coop.Management, Baroda.

Patel R.K.; Kumar P.; Gangadharan T.P.; Dhaka J.P.; Voegele K.; Srikumaran Nair R.; and Sreekumaran Nair G. (1976). Report of a Study of the Cattle Breeding Programme of Indo-Swiss Project, Kerala, NDRI, Karnal.

Pervaiz, Amir and Hendrik, C.K. (1989). "Conducting On-farm Animal Research: Procedures of Economic Analysis", Winrock International Institute for Agricultural Development and International Development Research Centre, USA & Canada.

Prasad, C.; Chowdhary, B.N.; and Bhatnagar, B. (1987). *First Line of Transfer of Technological Projects*. Publication and Information Division. ICAR, New Delhi.

Raman, K.V., Balaguru, T. and Manikanandan, P. (1988). *National Agricultural Research, Education and Extension Education System in India*. National Academy of Agricultural Research Management, Hyderabad.

Saroja, S. (1988). "Planning, Implementation and Evaluation of Agricultural Projects" (Ed.) Indian Institute of Public Administration, New Delhi.

Singh, K. (1987). *Managing Dairy Development Experiences and Lessons from Amul: Some Issues in Development Administration*, pp.142-166, Oxford & IBH Publishing co., New Delhi.

Singh, S.P. and Kelly, P.L. (1981). Amul—*An Experiment in Rural Economic Development*. Mac Millan, New Delhi.

Somzee, G. and Somzee, A.H. (1989). *Reaching Out to the Poor: The Unfinished Rural Revolution*. Mac Millan Press, U.K.

Subramanian, C. (1979). *The New Strategy in Indian Agriculture — The First Decade and After*. Vikas Publishing House, New Delhi p-85-86.

Supe, S.V. and Singh, S.N. (1969). *Dynamics of Rational Behaviour of Indian Farmers*. New Heights Publishers and Distributors, Delhi.

Ulrey, O. (1966). The Cooperative. An Agency for Rural Development (The Kaira District Cooperative Ltd., Anand, Gujarat State, India). Agricultural Economics Report No. 42, East Honsing, Michigan State University.

UN/FAO (1981). *World Food Programme*. Terminal Project Report, pp. 61-63.

Vaidyanathan, A (1989) : In *Livestock Economy of India*, Indian Society of Agricultural Economics, Oxford and IBH Publishing, New Delhi, pp. 1-43.

Venkatasubramanian, V. and Bandyopadhyay, A.K. (1998). *Agricultural Farming in Andaman and Nicobar Islands*, Technical Bulletin, Central Agricultural Research Institute, P.B. 181, Port Blair - 744101.

Venkatasubramanian, V. and Fulzele, R.M. (1996). *Dairy Farming in Tropics*, MD Publishers, New Delhi.

Venkateswarlu, K. and Kalla, J.C. (1996) *SWOT Analysis of NARP*, Delta Publishing House, 4, MCH Complex, Puttlibouli, Hyderabad-1.

Verhagen, M. (1990). Operation Flood and the Rural Poor. In : M. Doornbos and K.N. Nair (eds.). *Resources Institutions and Strategies : Operation Flood and Indian Dairying*, Sage Publications, New Delhi.

Index